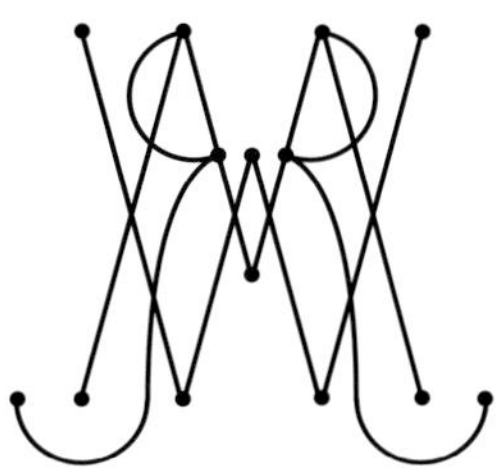

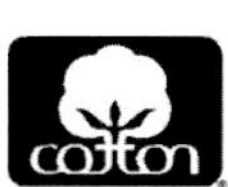

© 2009 Assouline Publishing
601 West 26th Street, 18th floor
New York, NY 10001, USA
Tel.: 212 989-6810   Fax: 212 647-0005
www.assouline.com

Color separation by Luc Alexis Chasleries

ISBN-13: 978-2759403998
Printed in Singapore

10 9 8 7 6 5 4 3 2 1

RUFFIAN
INSIDE OUT

INTRODUCTION BY NICOLE PHELPS

ASSOULINE

the "aha" moment for Ruffian's fall 2008 collection, (Re)form, came to designers Brian Wolk and Claude Morais when they were paging through a December 1939 *Vogue* and discovered a girls' boarding school directory. The classicism of New England preppies was appealing to Brian, who had attended the Rockland Country Day School in upstate New York, and to Claude, a vintage magazine fiend, but unlike the subjects of the photograph, the muse they had in mind was no straight-A student. She was a good girl gone bad, with one foot out the door and on the tour bus with her rock-star boyfriend—wearing a Christian Louboutin winter sandal, no less, a shoe her parents would never sanction. Culture versus counterculture is Brian and Claude's design mantra. It was writ large on their (Re)form inspiration board, where *Vogue* photos of Charles James dresses were juxtaposed with pictures of Kiss and Black Sabbath. And it came through in the collection's collaborations. After discovering Heather Dunbar's needlepoint pillows at The Future Perfect, a design store in their Williamsburg, Brooklyn neighborhood, Brian and Claude recruited her to create the needlepoint graffiti on several pieces, including their twisted take on a debutante dress. Strapless, short, and almost prim when viewed from a distance, upon closer inspection the dress had a waistband that looked like it had been lifted off the side of a 1970s subway car.

It wasn't long after their first date, in the fall of 2000—a reading of Marcel Proust's *In Search of Lost Time* at New York's National Arts Club (a seminal location for the duo)—that Brian and Claude began working together. Brian had been assisting Maggie Norris, the New York designer whose nascent label was influenced by her years as the design director at Ralph Lauren. When Brian introduced Claude to his boss, they instantly connected over their mutual passions for tailoring and luxurious fabrics. Claude calls the three seasons they collaborated with Norris his master's degree.

"Research and sketching are the foundation of our work; they help us understand a woman's emotional connection to clothing and silhouettes," says Brian. While other young labels go straight from drawings to fabric, Brian and Claude do muslins. This sets Ruffian apart. Why go to the extra expense of not one, but two, muslin fittings? "We get to see what it's going to look like on the human form," explains Claude. "We work out a lot of mistakes at this stage. You can send a drawing to the seamstress and the piece itself can come back totally different than how you imagined it." For Pomp, their spring 2008 collection, they were playing with ruffles—at the neckline, cascading down the side of the body, marching up the arms—so it was more important than ever to make sure the fit was perfect.

A lecture on Madame de Pompadour at the National Arts Club was the genesis of Pomp. The designers were attracted to the independence of this self-made Frenchwoman, a courtesan and mistress to Louis XV, and they made her rebellious aesthetic the key influence of their collection. As spot-on as that was—romance and florals would become big spring trends—Brian and Claude weren't content with a single, straightforward reference. As their second muse, they chose another era's rebel, Blondie's Debbie Harry, who, with the imminent and lamented closing of New York's seminal punk club, CBGB, was frequently in the news when they were working on the collection. It was an inspired pairing. The parallels between the women's styles of dress are obvious to students of fashion. Madame de Pompadour had her ruffles, bows and ruching. For Debbie Harry, it was studs and safety pins and zippers.

After the fittings, they cut the fabric. Of course, a dress can come back from the seamstress looking nothing like it did in muslin. "Some things work out, some things don't," says Claude. "Sometimes fabulous mistakes happen." During the making of Pomp, he explains, a black silk trench with a ruffle collar was returned with its hem unfinished exposing the hot-pink piping that was meant to be turned under. "We left it out, and it was fabulous." So fabulous that Jada Pinkett Smith wore the piece to the premiere of *I Am Legend*.

Ruffian can trace its beginnings to when Brian's father bought him a sewing machine. He was twelve years old. While attending school, he took Saturday classes in Manhattan at the Fashion Institute of Technology; after graduating he studied fashion at FIT and costume design at Purchase College at the State University of New York. Two summers at the Santa Fe Opera in New Mexico—"I'm secretly a bohemian, but it doesn't show," he says—inspired his first collection of ruffs. The collars were made of lace, velvet, chiffon, and silk organza; some were soft, others architectural; some were small and pleated, others rivaled those of Elizabeth I in their size and flamboyance. Indeed, with the film *Elizabeth* coming out in theaters, Brian's timing couldn't have been better. His Fashion Week presentation in late 1998 at the Gramercy Park home of his childhood friend, Typhaine Zagoreos, caught the attention of the influential British stylist Isabella Blow (who has since passed away), who used the ruffs in a shoot for the *Sunday London Times*. At the same time, Karl Lagerfeld himself shot Cate Blanchett wearing one for *Harper's Bazaar*. Ruffian was born.

The New York fashion landscape in 1999 was far friendlier to new designers than it is today. "It was easy to get a slot on the fashion calendar," laughs Brian. He had to pinch himself when his white ribbon ruff landed in the Madison Avenue windows of Barneys New York—and on the cover of the store's catalog. "I naively sent them the entire first collection, and they bought them all." Liberty of London and a shop in Japan also picked them up, but Brian remained a one-man show. "It was just me and my fax machine in my apartment," he says. Meanwhile, the Lagerfeld *Bazaar* shoot had led to a job as an accessories consultant for Chanel in Paris.

While Brian was working at the company's famous rue Cambon headquarters, Claude was living as a stylist in Paris. A French Canadian born in Montreal, he left home at seventeen, before graduating from high school, to model. His tall, lean frame won him steady runway work in Milan, Tokyo, and the City of Lights. A decade in front of the camera for the likes of Paul Smith, Christian Dior, and Yohji Yamamoto segued into a career behind it. His clients included Tina Brown's magazine *Talk*, *Elle*, Toronto's *Fashion*, and the Canadian department store Holt Renfrew.

around the time Brian and Claude sent their fabrics to the seamstress for Pomp, they had a meeting with jewelry designer Dana Lorenz, of Fenton. In keeping with the collection's Madame de Pompadour-meets-Debbie Harry theme, they wanted jewelry that looked hard yet classic. Lorenz worked with whitewashed gold and antique silver, and combined studs with Swarovski crystals and pearls. A meeting with Christian Louboutin established the direction for the shoes. Collectively they decided on a small toe box, as it seemed evocative of eighteenth-century France, while a hidden platform and vertiginous heel made the shoes modern.

After determining the jewelry and shoes came hair and makeup, followed by advice from their stylist Natasha Royt, and support from their show sponsors M.A.C and Bumble & bumble. "It's like the third trimester," says Brian. "Suddenly, your baby is everybody's baby. Everybody's got opinions." Including the models. Brian and Claude like brainy beauties, and if they're brunette, even better. "I'm particularly fond of Irina because we share the same hometown and language," Claude says of Irina Lazareanu, who opened Ruffian's shows for two seasons running and would have done so a third time for Pomp if a Saturday-afternoon traffic jam hadn't prevented her from arriving on time. "She understands the counterculture element of our style, yet still possesses the intellectual raffiné that embodies our woman." Lisa Cant wore the collection's dramatic "One Wing Dove" dress. "She has the perfect line," says Brian. And then there are her absolutely hypnotic blue eyes, which stood out all the more against the hot pink of her frock. Like Pomp's clothes and accessories, the show's beauty look was at once hard and soft. Stylist Neil Moodie's French twist was piled high in the front like a pompadour, but the look was more rockabilly than rococo. On the morning of the show, the air conditioning in the National Arts Club broke down, bringing forth the period quality of the models' makeup—Polly Osmond had dusted their faces with loose powder above their hairline and painted their lips a Sèvres-porcelain pink—into sharp relief.

not long after September 11, 2001, with an initial investment of two hundred dollars each, Brian and Claude launched a collection of men's neckties in couture fabrics. It was hardly a get-rich-quick scheme, but once again the creations were shipped off to Barneys, and once again the buyer snapped them up.

Ruffian was reborn as a duo in 2002. Originally a play on the word "ruff," the name stuck even though Brian and Claude quickly broadened the scope of the collection beyond neckwear. At the request of their contact at Barneys, they added women's organza boleros to the line, followed by soft bead necklaces of the kind popularized by Prada and Lanvin. Sometimes a client—inevitably someone from Grand Rapids or Dallas—will ask if the label is named after Ruffian, one of the greatest female racehorses of all time. Actually, it's nothing but an amusing coincidence. Brian and Claude take pleasure in the simple fact that their refined, elegant clothes are sold under a name that implies quite the opposite.

On a trip to London, the boys met with their first fan, Isabella Blow. She connected them with Nadja Swarovski, who took one look at their pieces and said, "I want to sponsor a show." It was decision time. Brian and Claude couldn't continue working for Norris and simultaneously design their own collection. They made the split. For Ruffian's first show in February, 2002, Swarovski offered Brian and Claude sponsorship funds and had a chandelier shipped from the crystal company's Austrian headquarters to New York for the occasion. At Beethoven Hall on East Fifth Street, with a pianist for accompaniment, they showed a focused collection of thirteen nearly identical little black dresses (only the silhouettes of the sleeves changed) with thirteen different neckpieces and collars.

r ather than simply reprinting that 1939 *Vogue* boarding-school directory, Brian and Claude decided to doodle on it like a teenager would. After several failed attempts at mimicking the bubble script that then as now articulates the sugar-spun angst of American girlhood, they enlisted a friend, the artist Anne Koch, to transform the directory into a rebellious tapestry with hot-pink scribbles. She drew a scary cat over the Salem School, piles of coins over the Knox School, and a crown over Kingswood-Cranbrook. (Re)form included white collared boys' shirts trimmed with French lace cuffs; the duo's own skinny ties that emphasized the collection's long, lean silhouette; and a belt buckle inspired by a vintage find at the Arkansas State Fair (They removed the center and inserted Ruffian's logo crest).

Another tiny detail that Brian and Claude delighted in, which likely went unnoticed by all but their most ardent fans, and then only those sitting in the front row: the "Creative Nail" manicure team painted the models' fingernails and then chipped them in places so that they looked like authentic private-school coeds with burgeoning bad-girl streaks. Makeup artist James Kaliardos, who's best known for his work with Chanel and Balenciaga, did an ultraviolet lip, the thinking being that lipstick is the first thing girls experiment with when they begin to wear makeup. The show's venue, New Dance Group Studios, was across the street from Brian and Claude's Garment District atelier. Convenient, yes. But also a perfect fit for the collection, dance being such an important, almost symbolic element in American girls' upbringing.

With its single-malt-hued wood paneling, the National Arts Club's masculinity married the violets and nudes of a French boudoir with the acid green associated with punk. Brian and Claude hung hot-pink Venetian drapes sourced from a Hollywood rental company, at the back of the runway. The drapes had been used in *The Women*, George Cukor's 1939 film starring Norma Shearer, Joan Crawford, and Rosalind Russell. A more inspired provenance is hard to imagine—the French government let Sofia Coppola shoot *Marie Antoinette* on the grounds of Versailles, but it's not in the business of lending furniture.

Brian and Claude live on the parlor floor of a town house in Williamsburg, Brooklyn, built in 1880. Their apartment is an inspired mix of reupholstered antique furniture and thrift-store finds like old LPs and vintage paint-by-numbers pictures. Outside, their 1994 Jeep is parked in the empty lot. Claude is an avid magazine collector, but he's generally the more monastic of the two. The peripatetic life of a model taught him the beauty of a white room, an army cot, and a single suitcase. Brian is more baroque, more apt to put things up on the walls. Physically, too, they're perfect foils. With his green eyes, olive skin, and closely shaved head, Claude is several inches taller than Brian, who has perpetually tousled brown hair through which he constantly runs his hands. Most days Claude sports a soft, faded T-shirt and broken-in jeans or thin-wale cords. In the colder months he might add a shrunken thrift-store sweater. Brian is a bit more of a dandy; he's taken his bow in a pin-striped shorts suit.

the division of labor isn't as black and white, but these are the things that they agree on: Claude has a great sense of color; Brian has a good sense of surface and is interested in form. Still there can be a lot of friction. They finish each other's sentences more often than they disagree, but when Brian and Claude do argue, it's always about the same things: Young versus old, uptown versus downtown, pleasing the editors versus satisfying the retailers. The dichotomies are integral to their aesthetic. "We're obsessed with contrast and clash," says Brian. In Pomp it was princesses and punks. In (Re)form it was the prep and the rebel. "We're interested in the anthropology of fashion—why something was worn and what it meant within the zeitgeist," continues Claude. "We use those elements in a postmodern way to see what they mean when they're re-contextualized in our contemporary cultural consciousness." That means a tuxedo jacket comes not in black but in metallic tweed, and a boyfriend jacket in the most precious plaid bouclé. When one of those tuxedos was featured on Vogue.com, Brian and Claude racked up multiple sales, proof that this postmodern experiment of theirs is producing modern, desirable clothes.

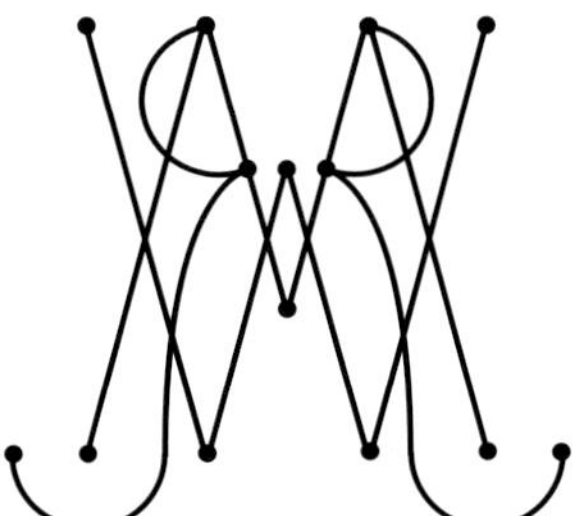

"We're interested in the anthropology of fashion, why something was worn and what it meant within the zeitgeist."

—RUFFIAN

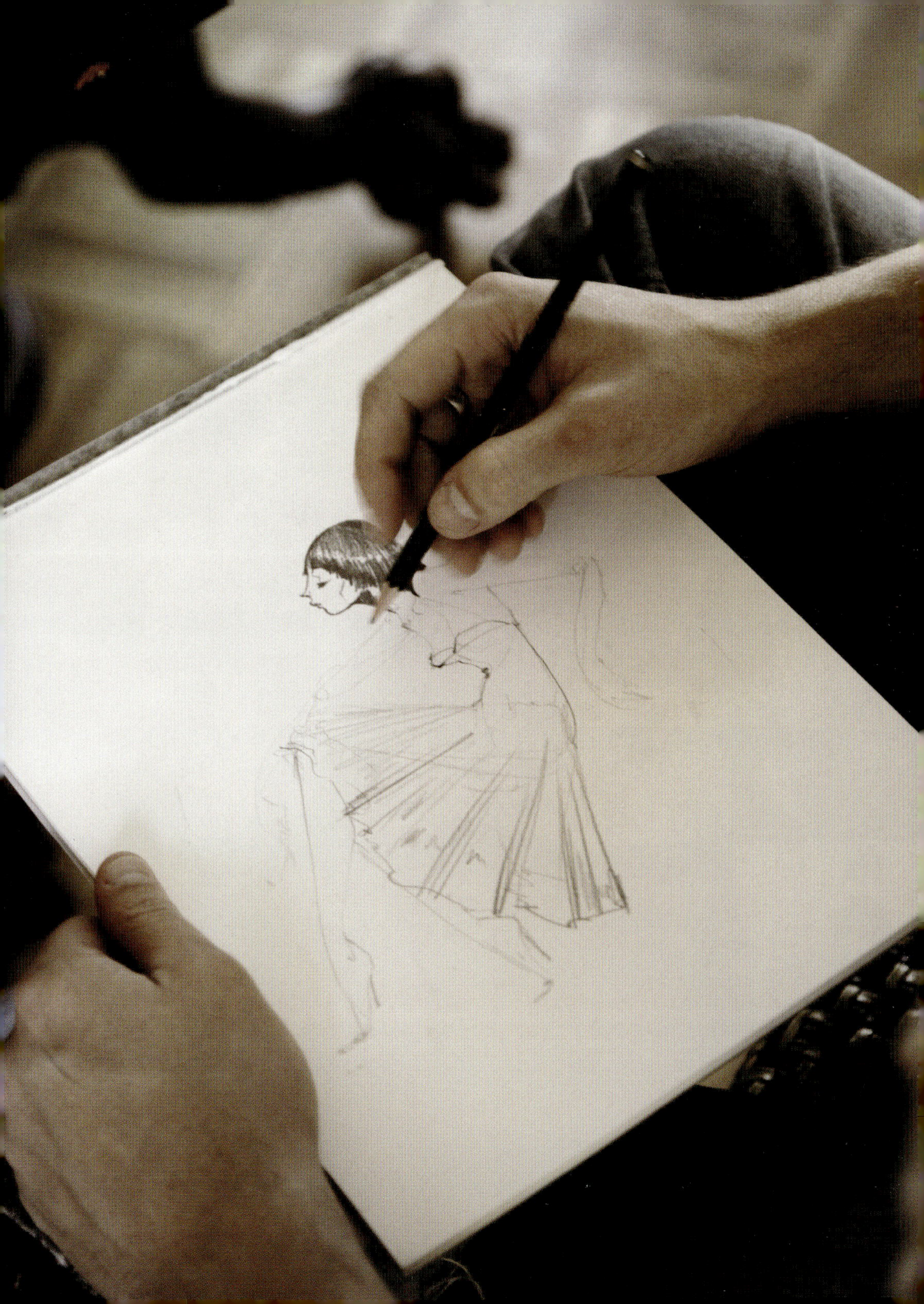

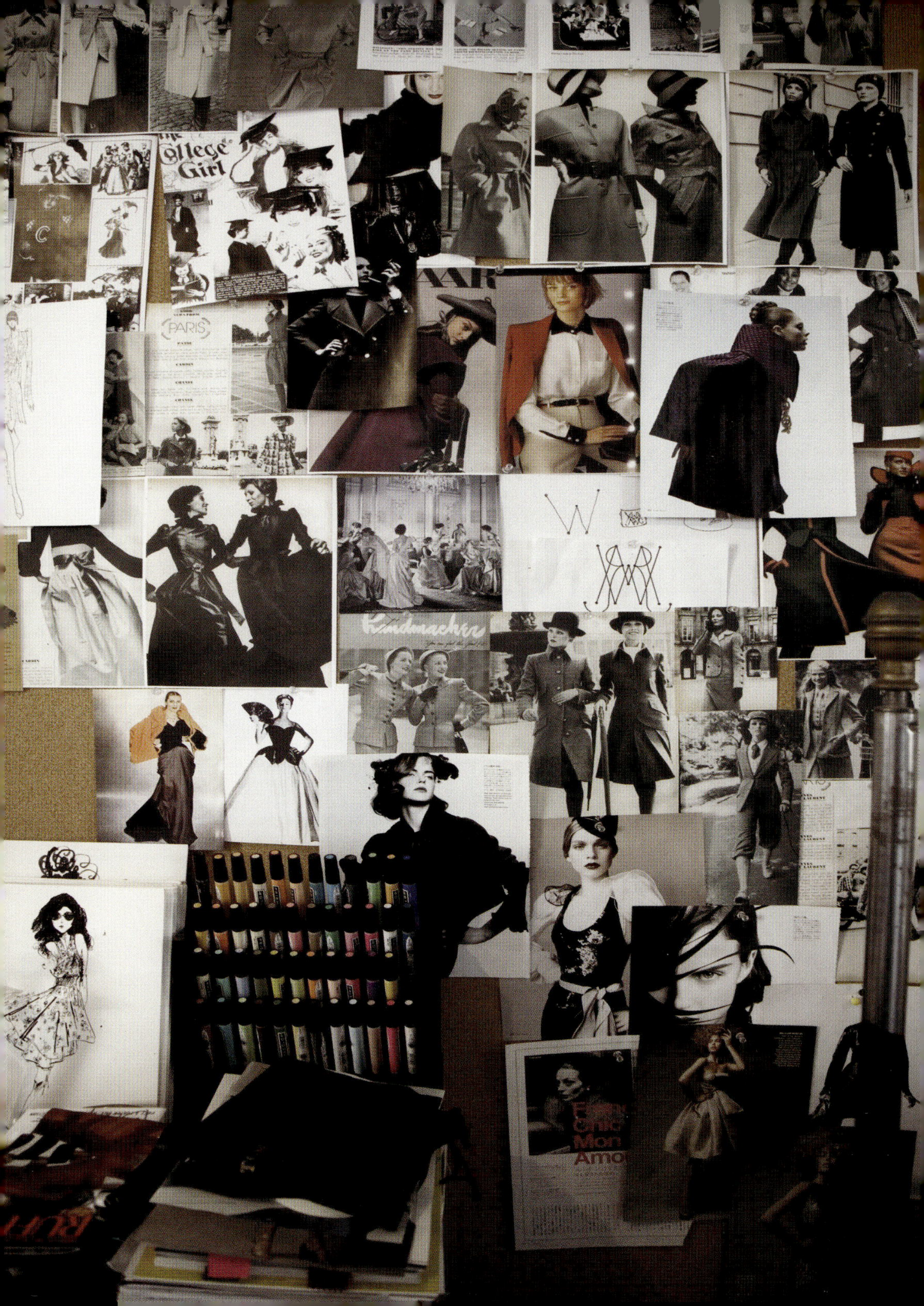

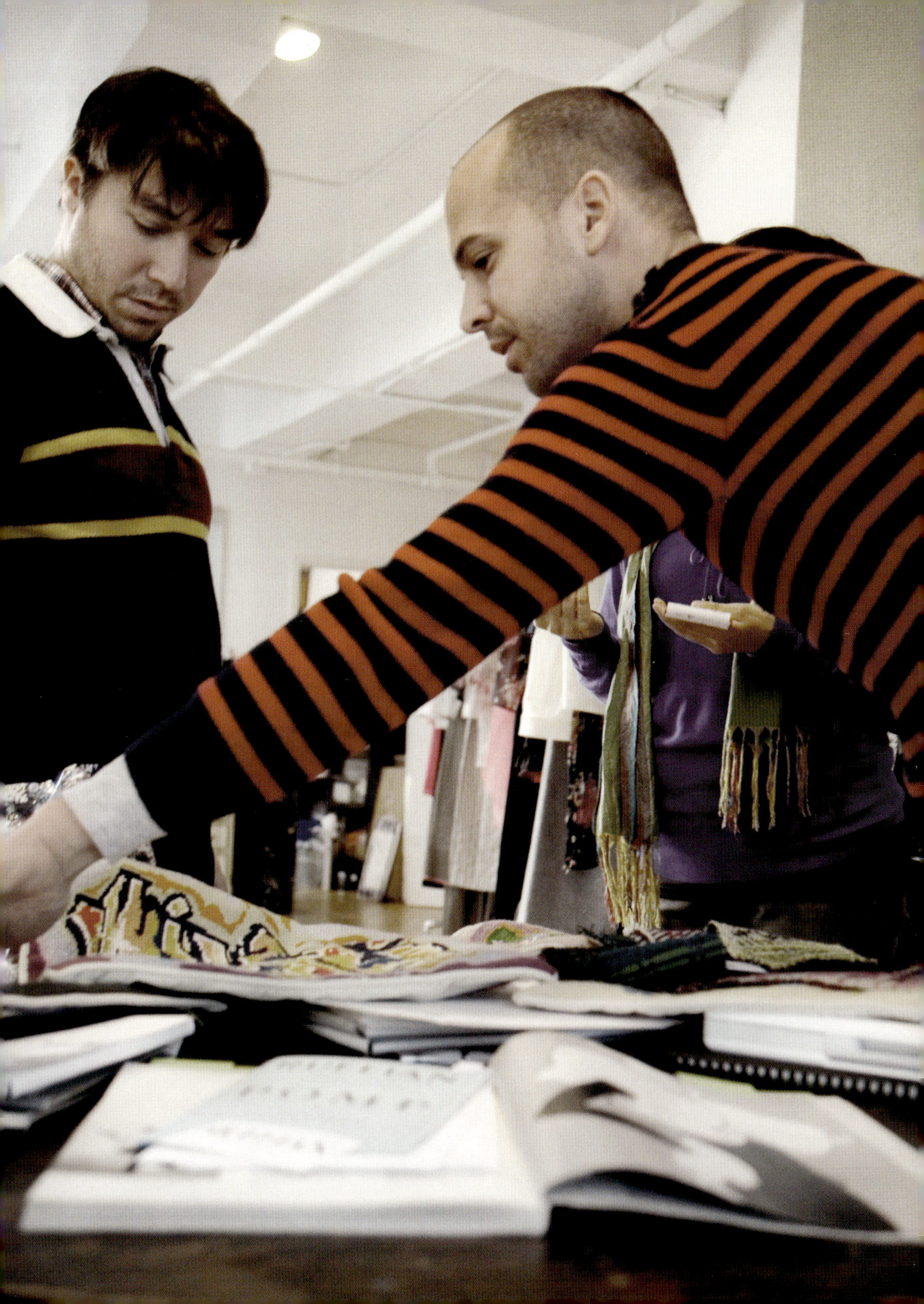

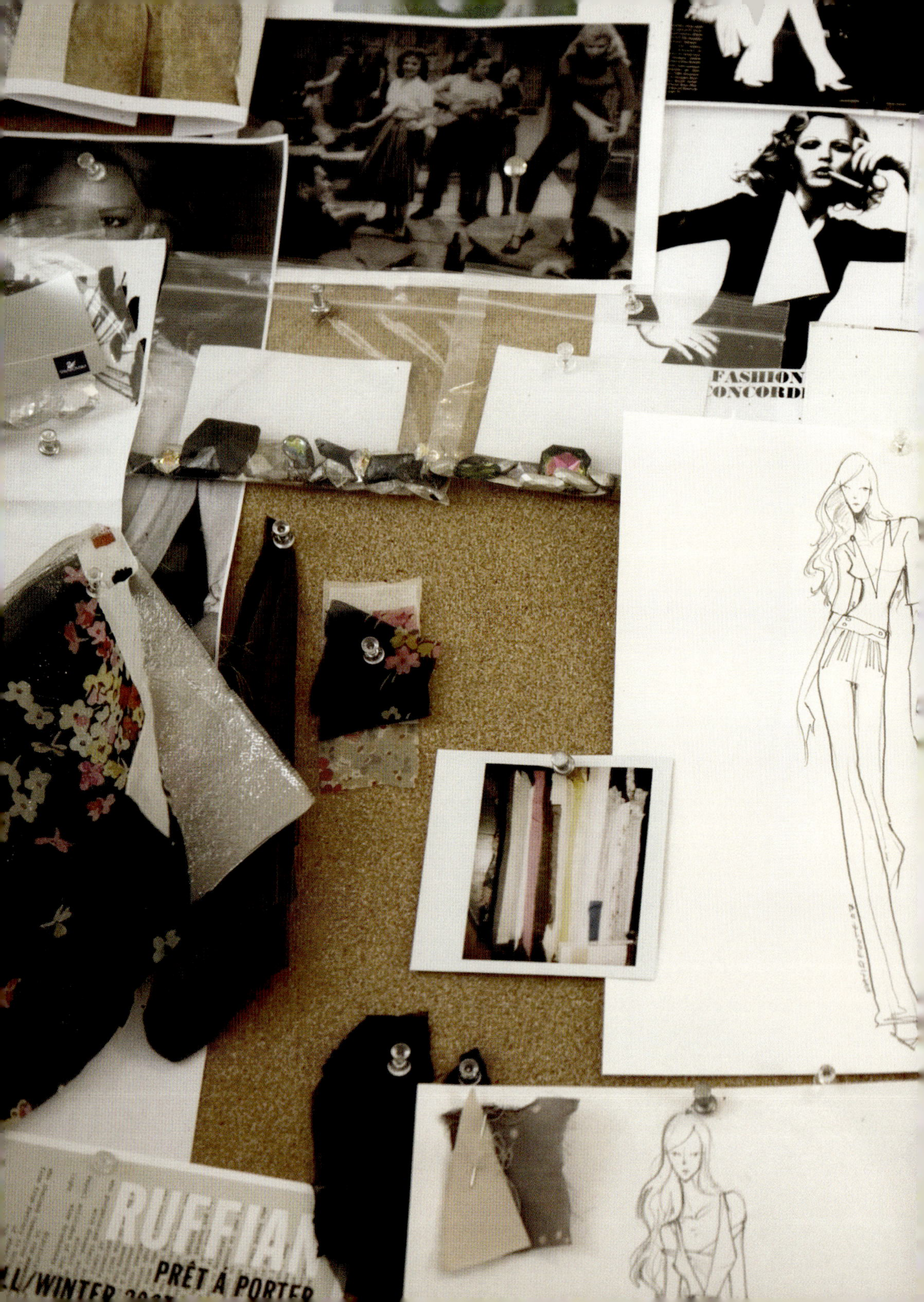
FASHION
CONCORDE
RUFFIAN
PRÊT À PORTER
FALL/WINTER 200

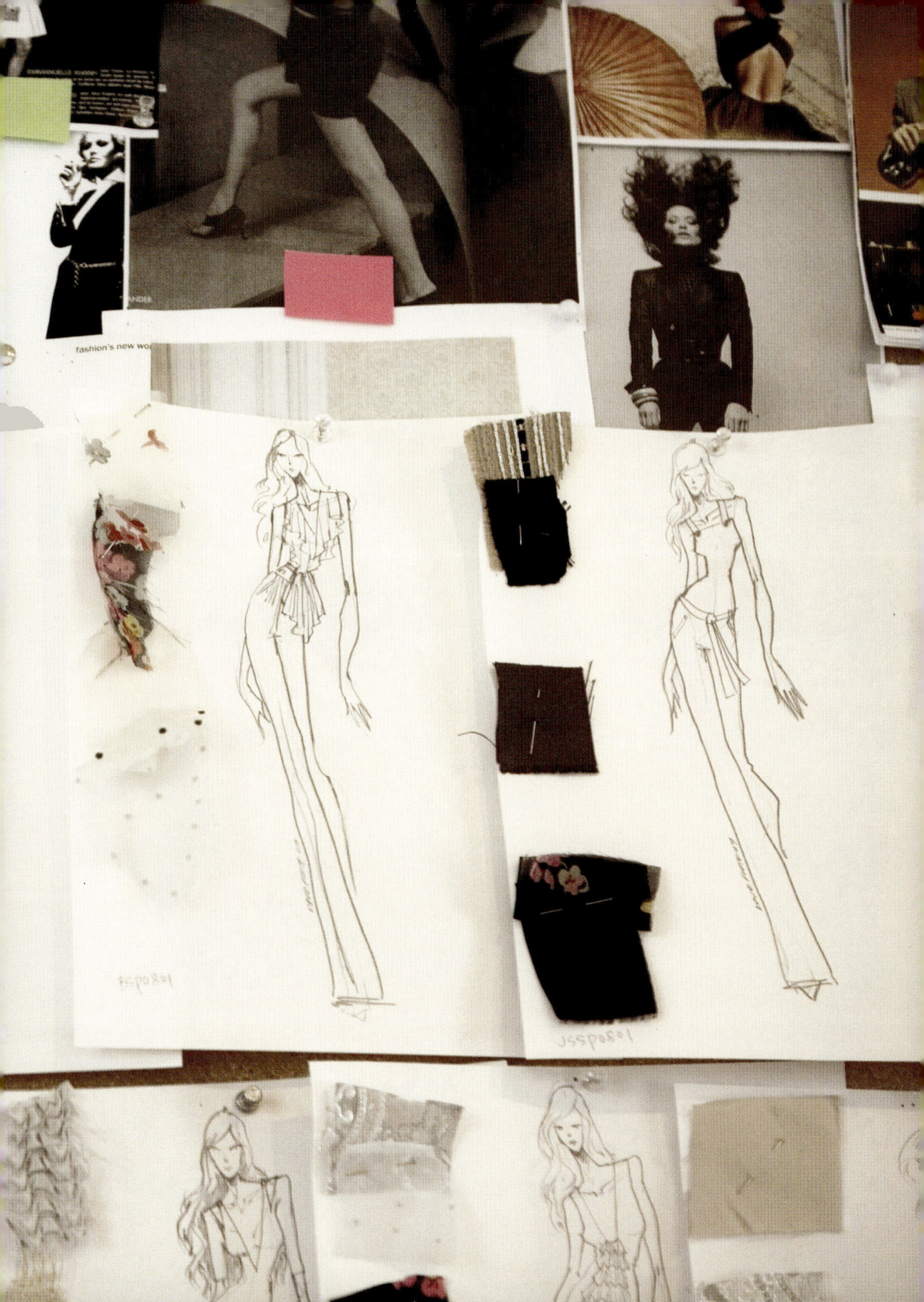

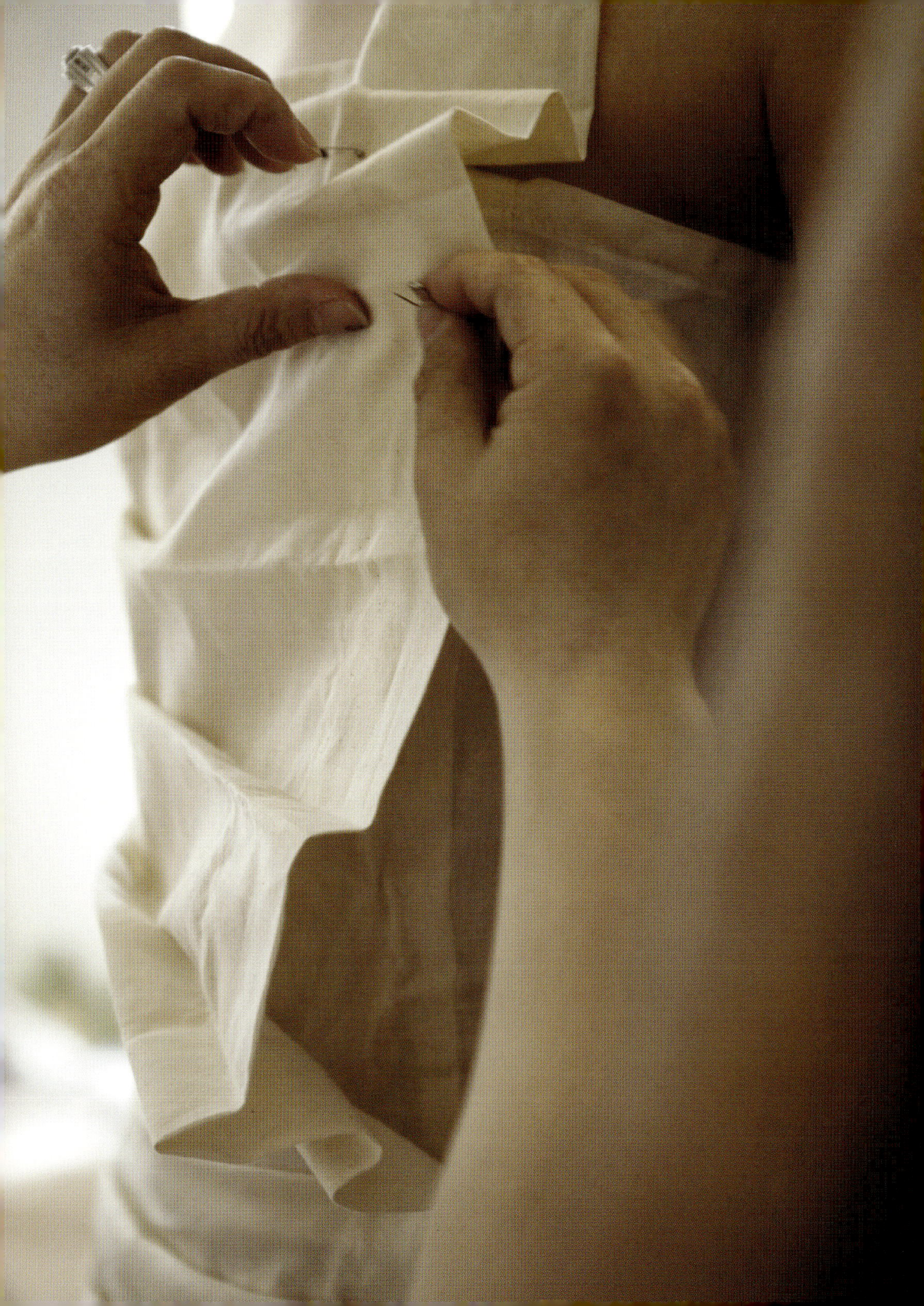

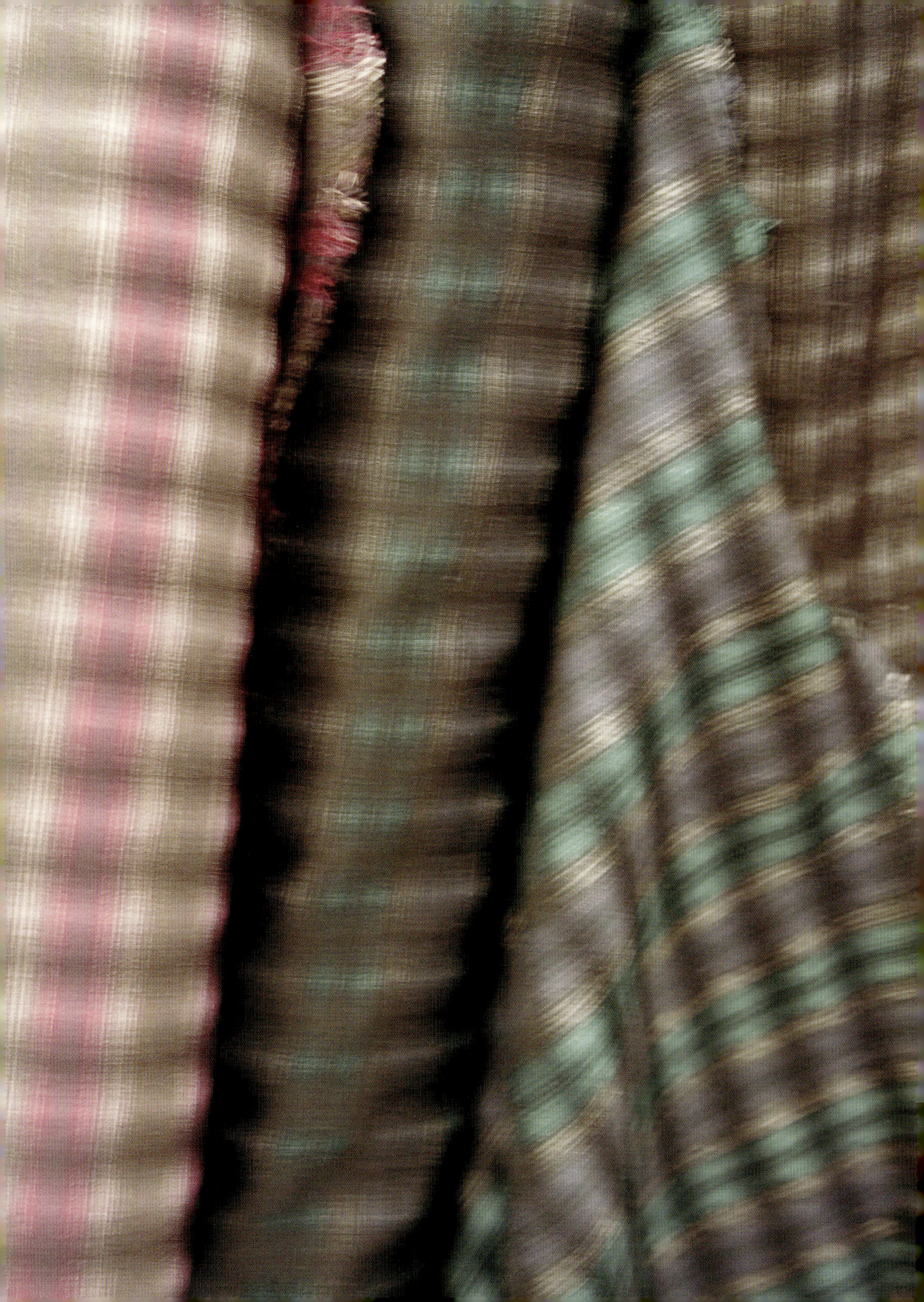

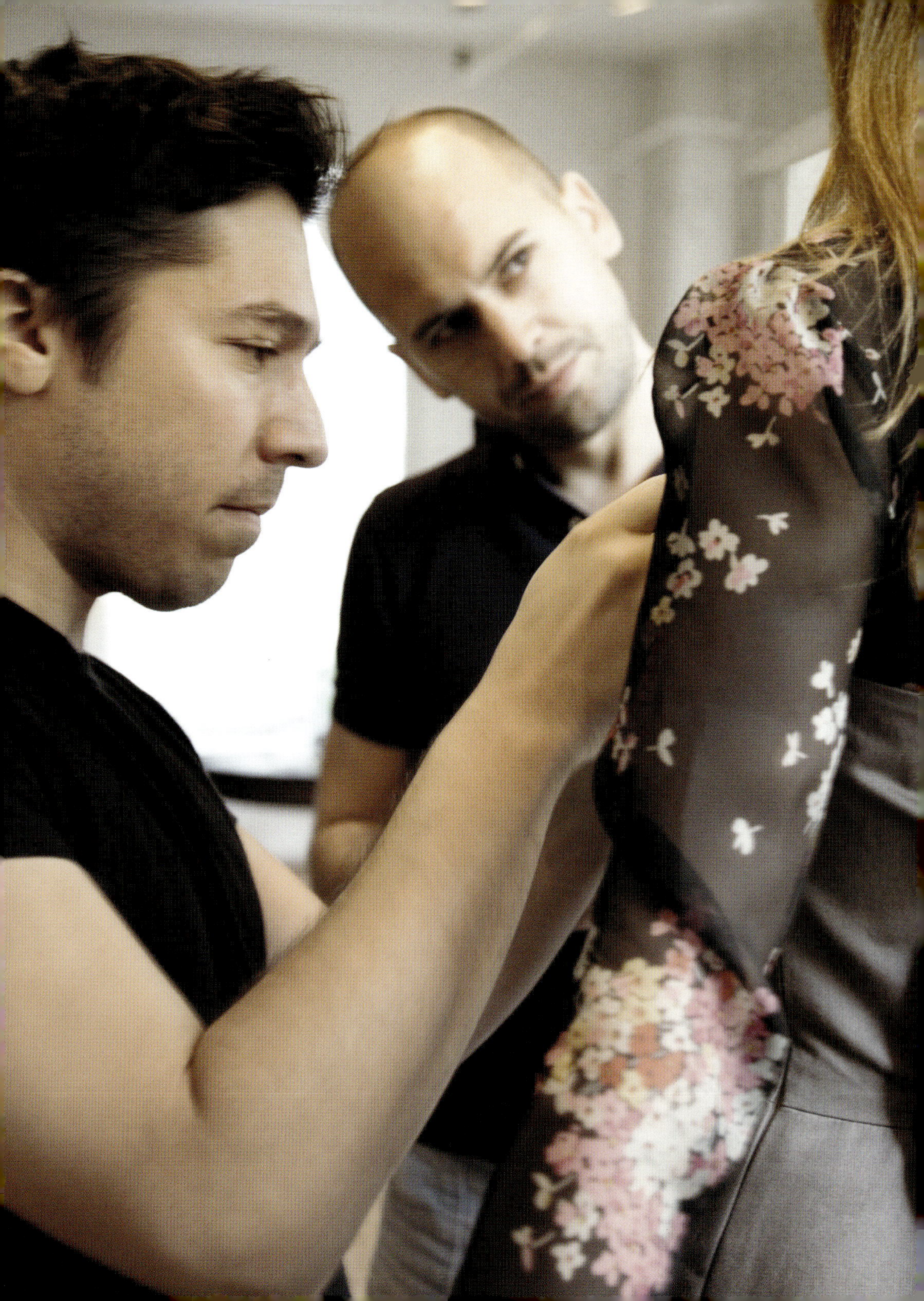

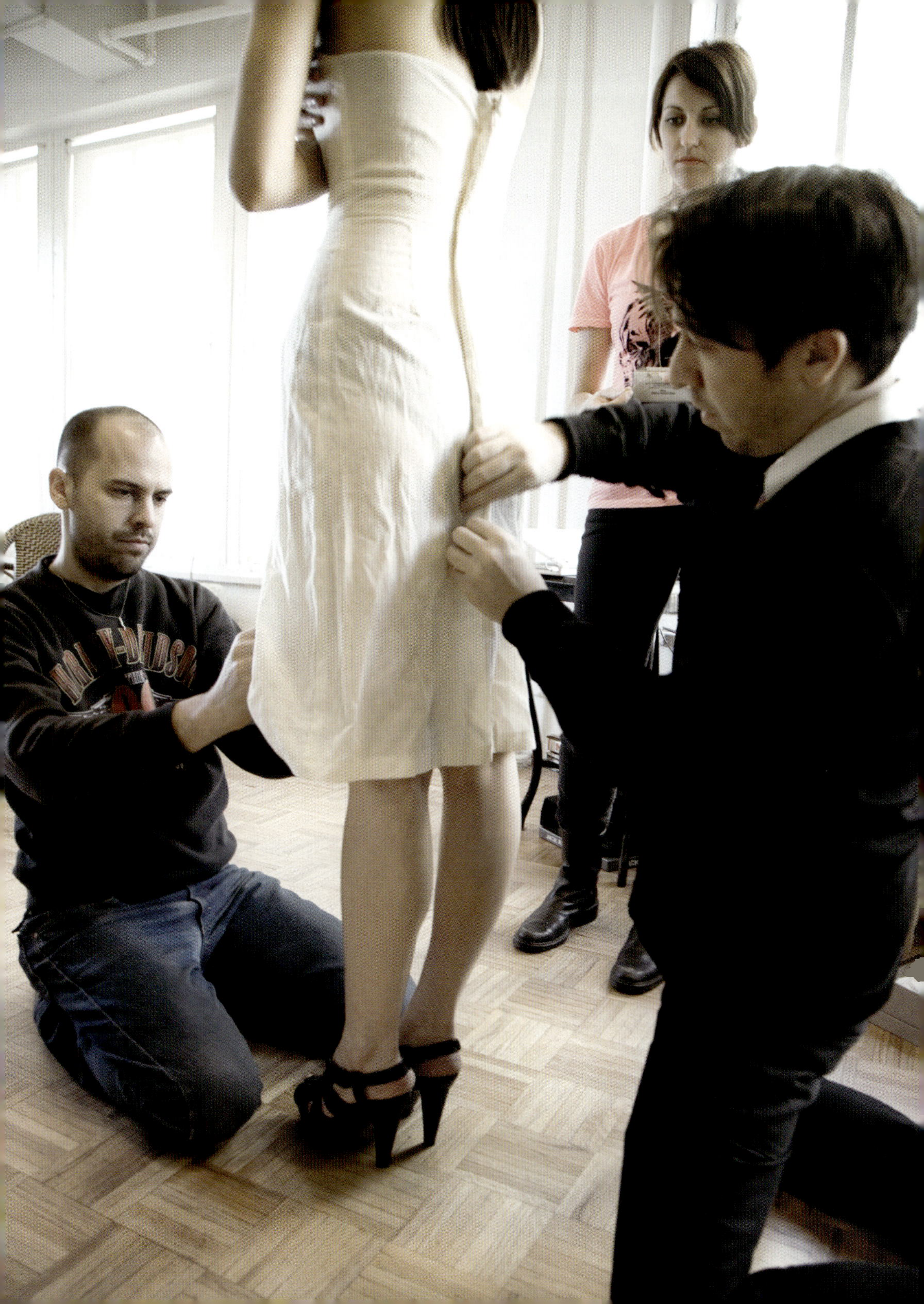

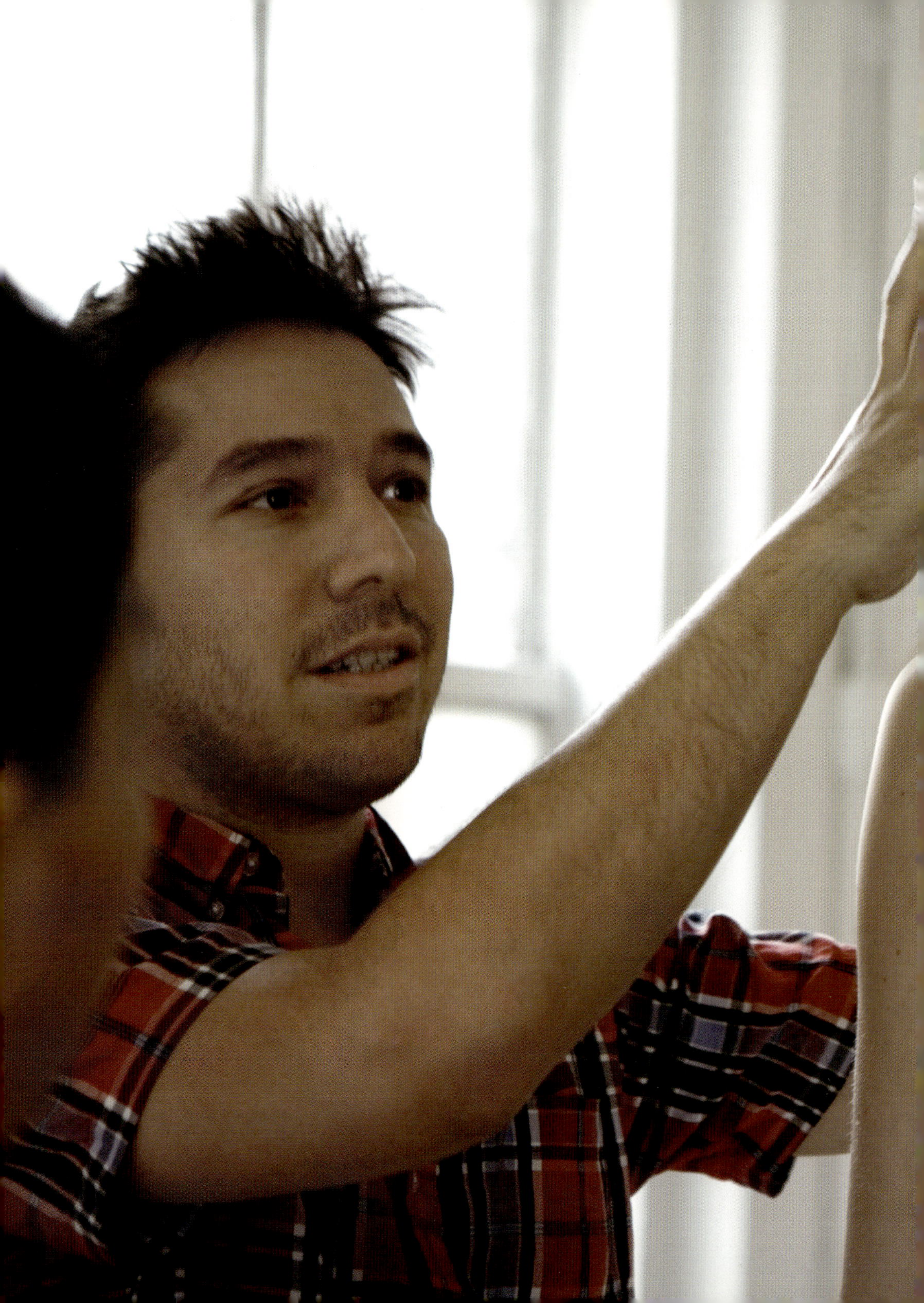

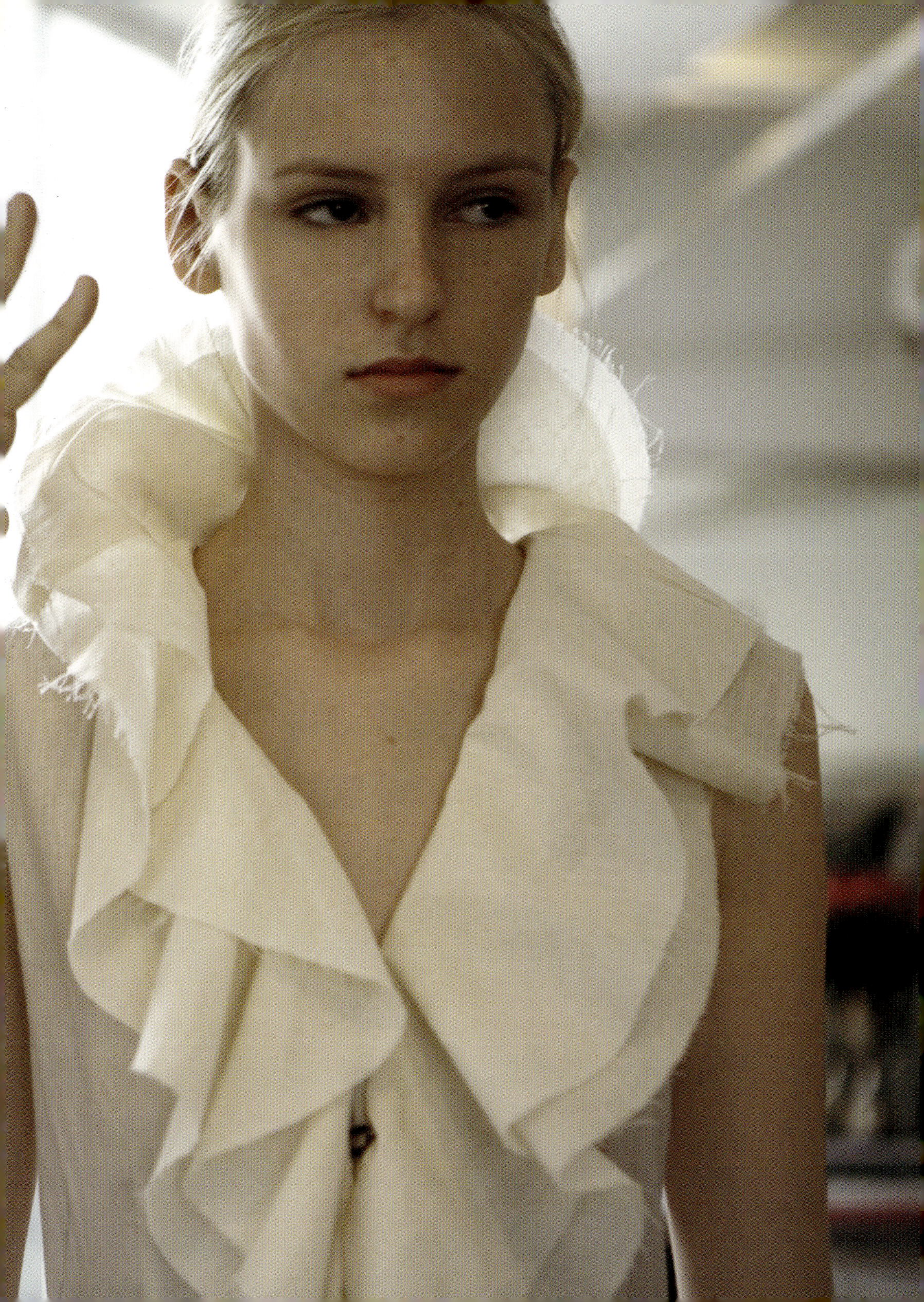

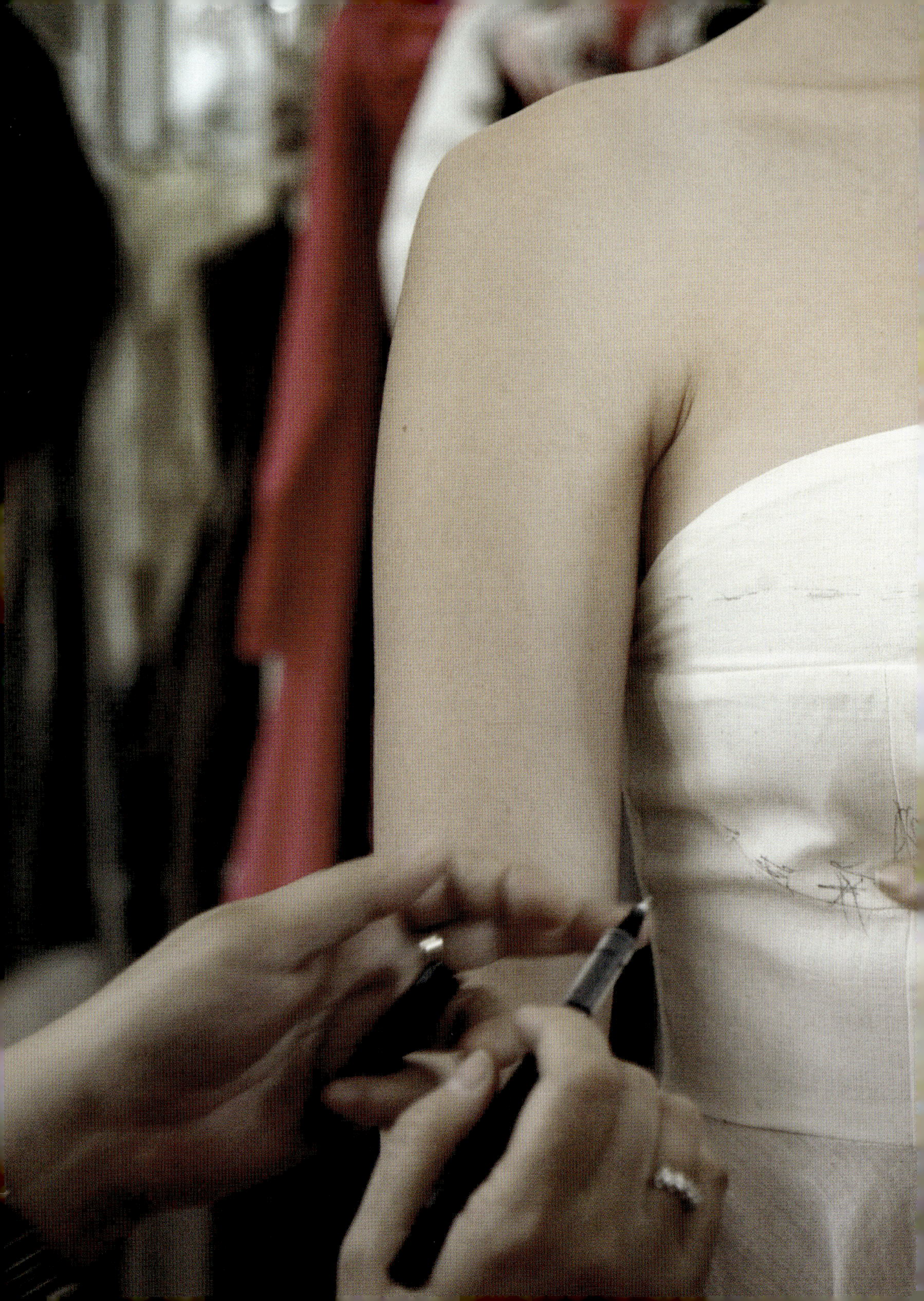

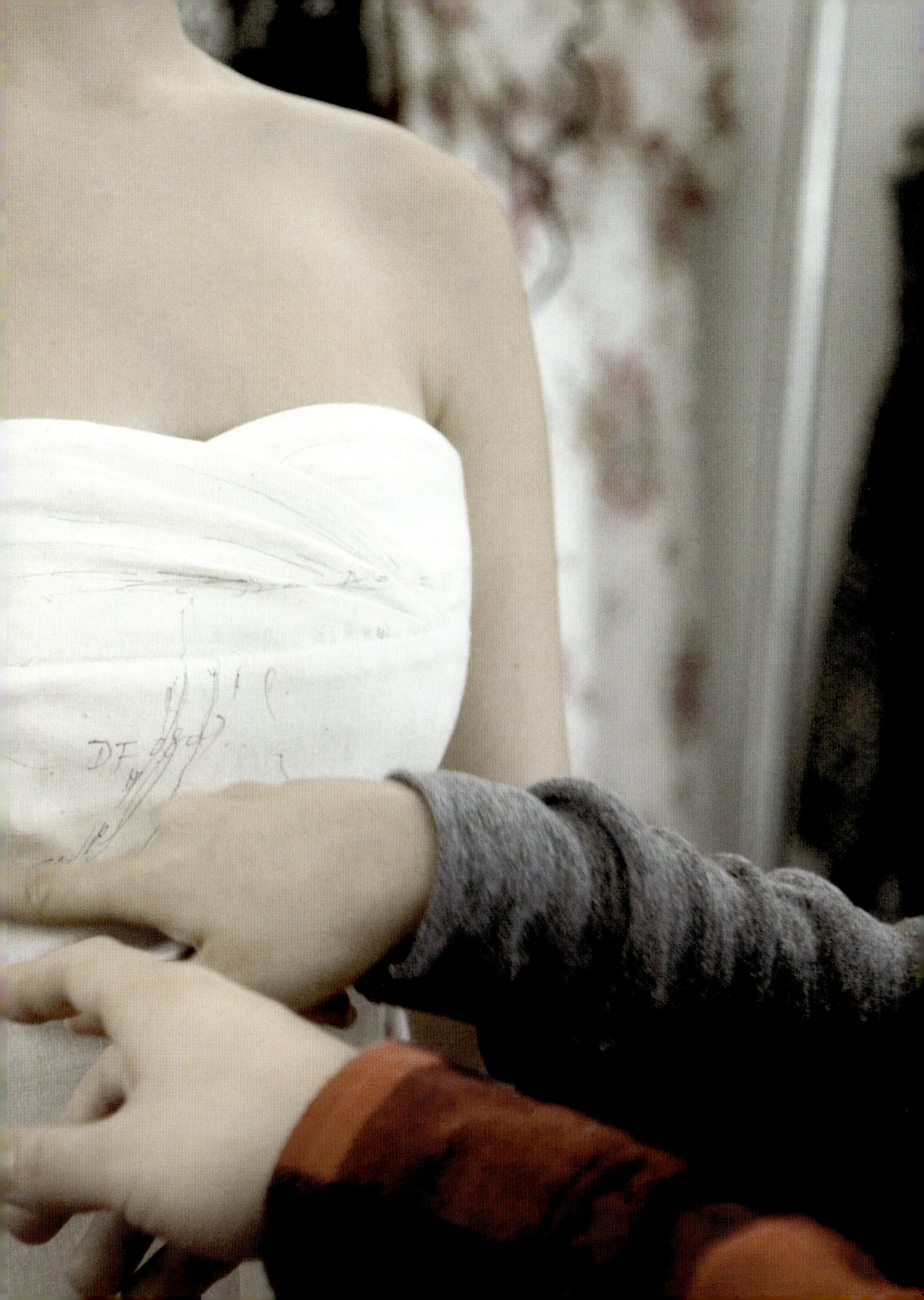

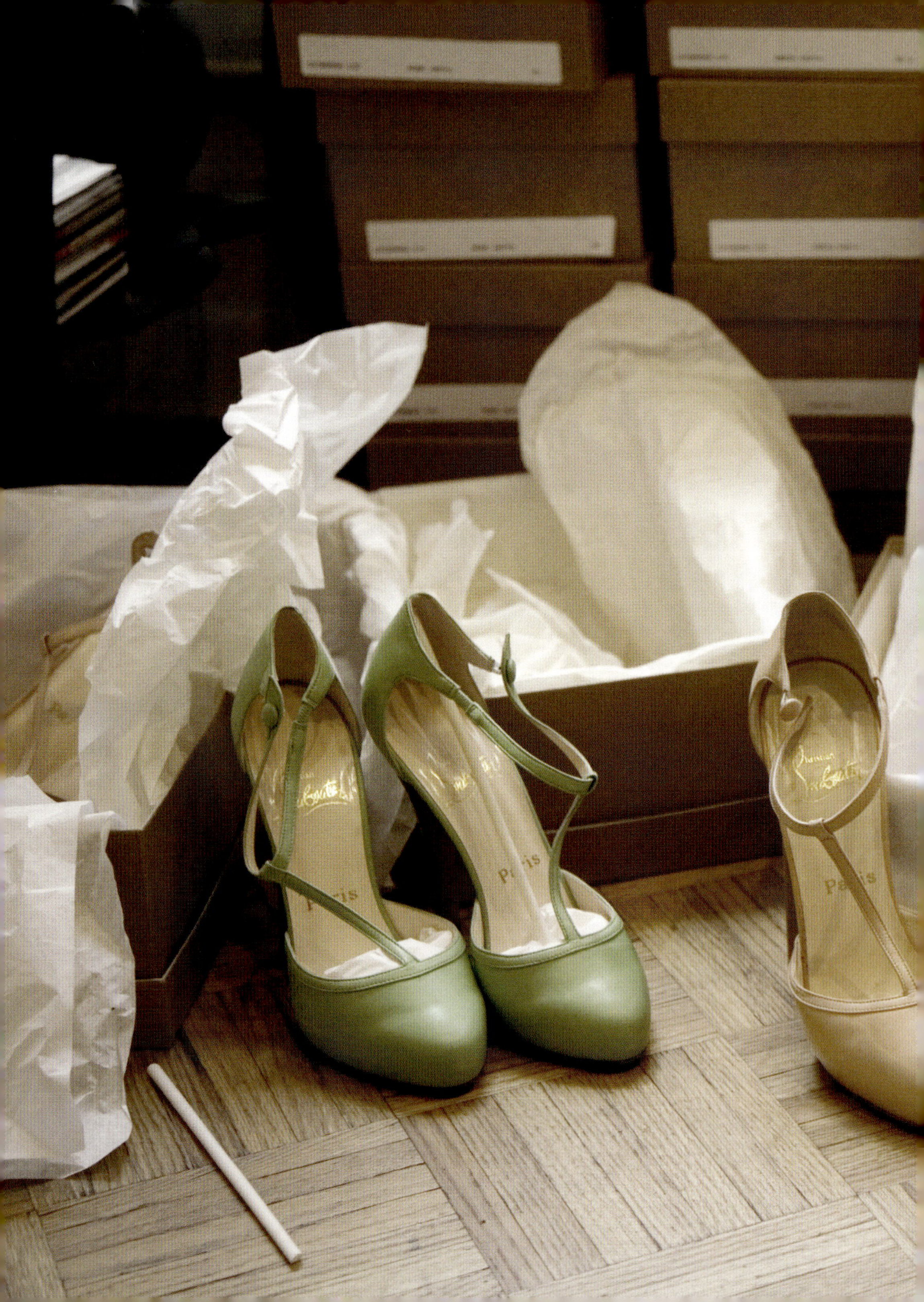

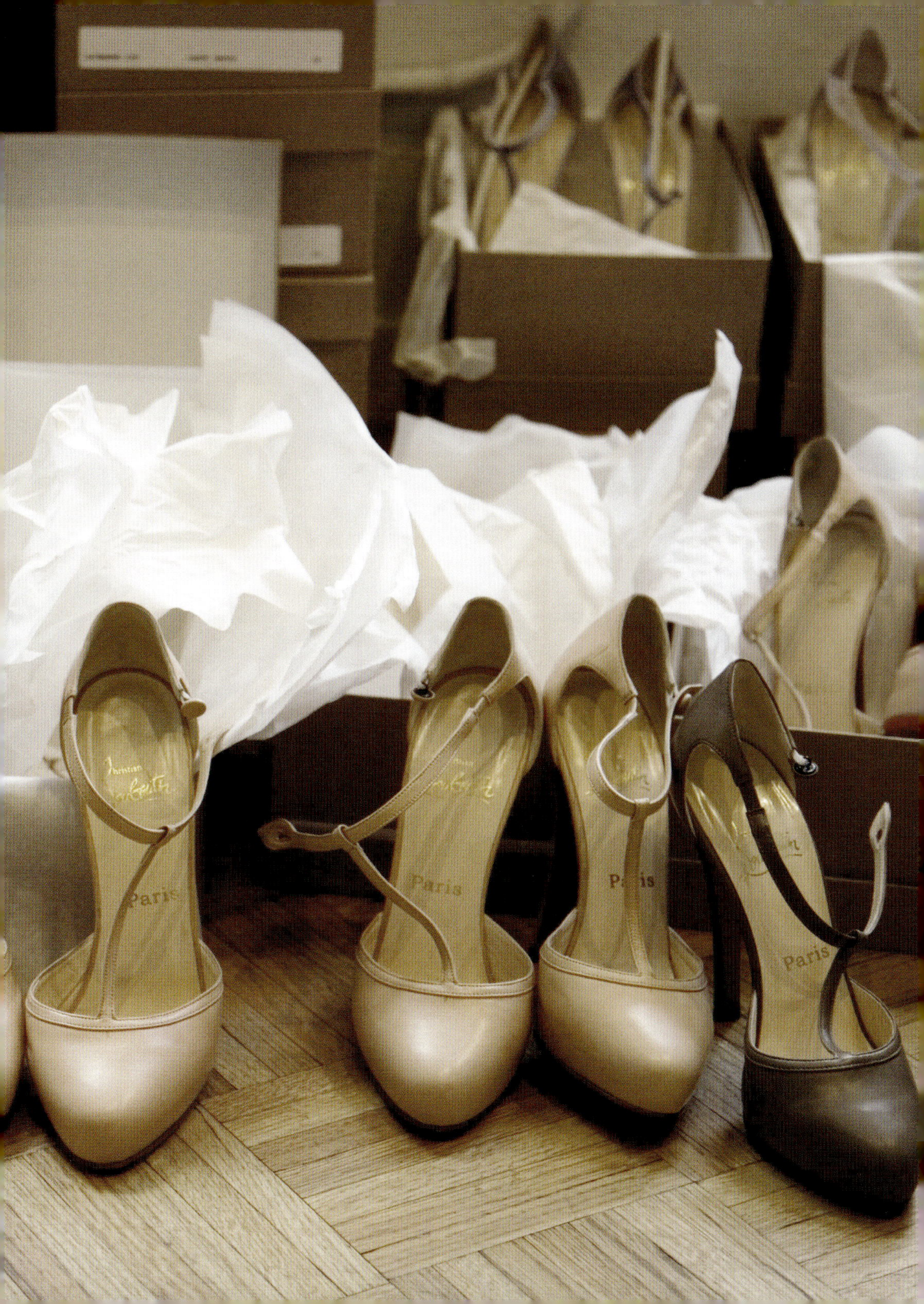

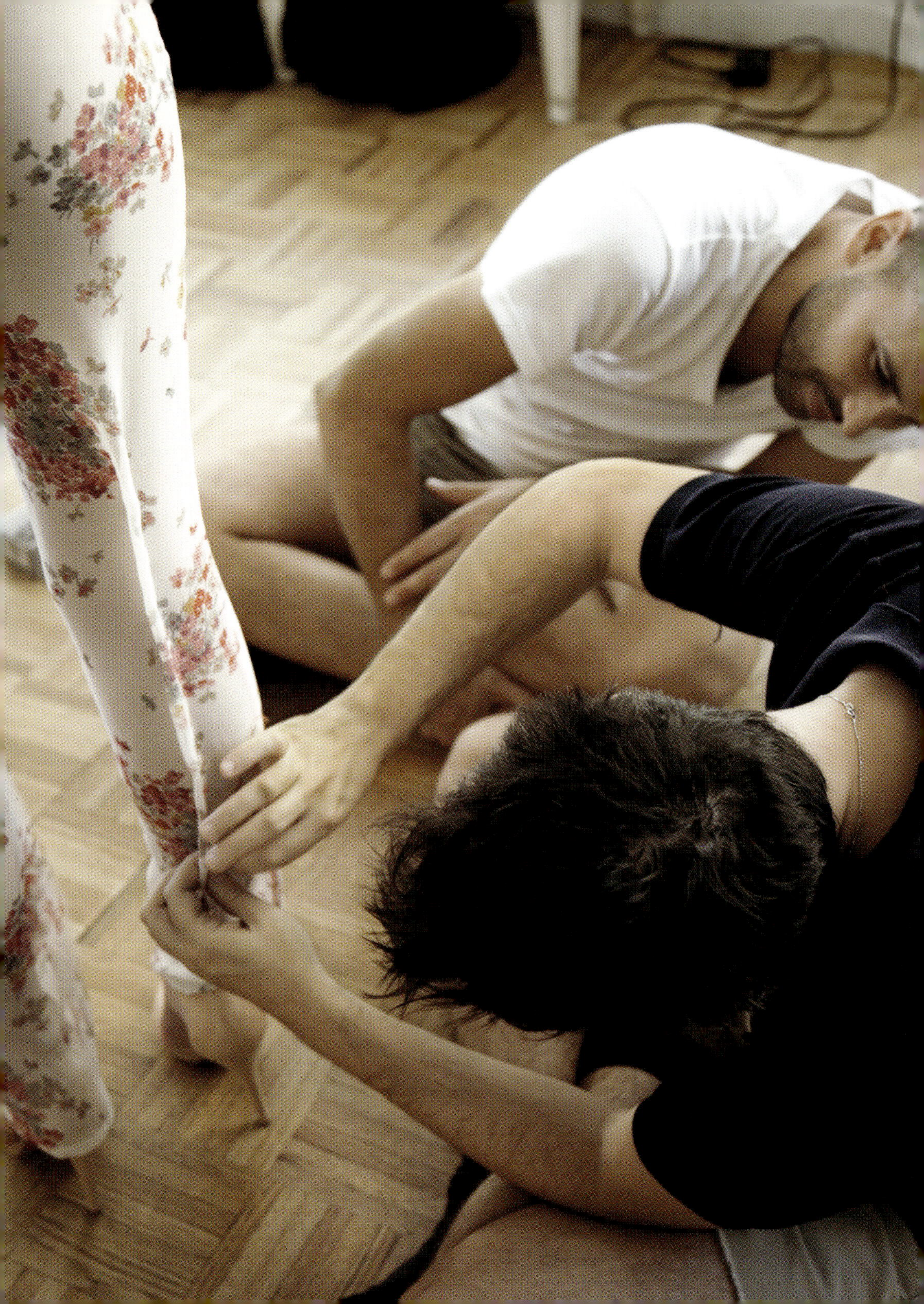

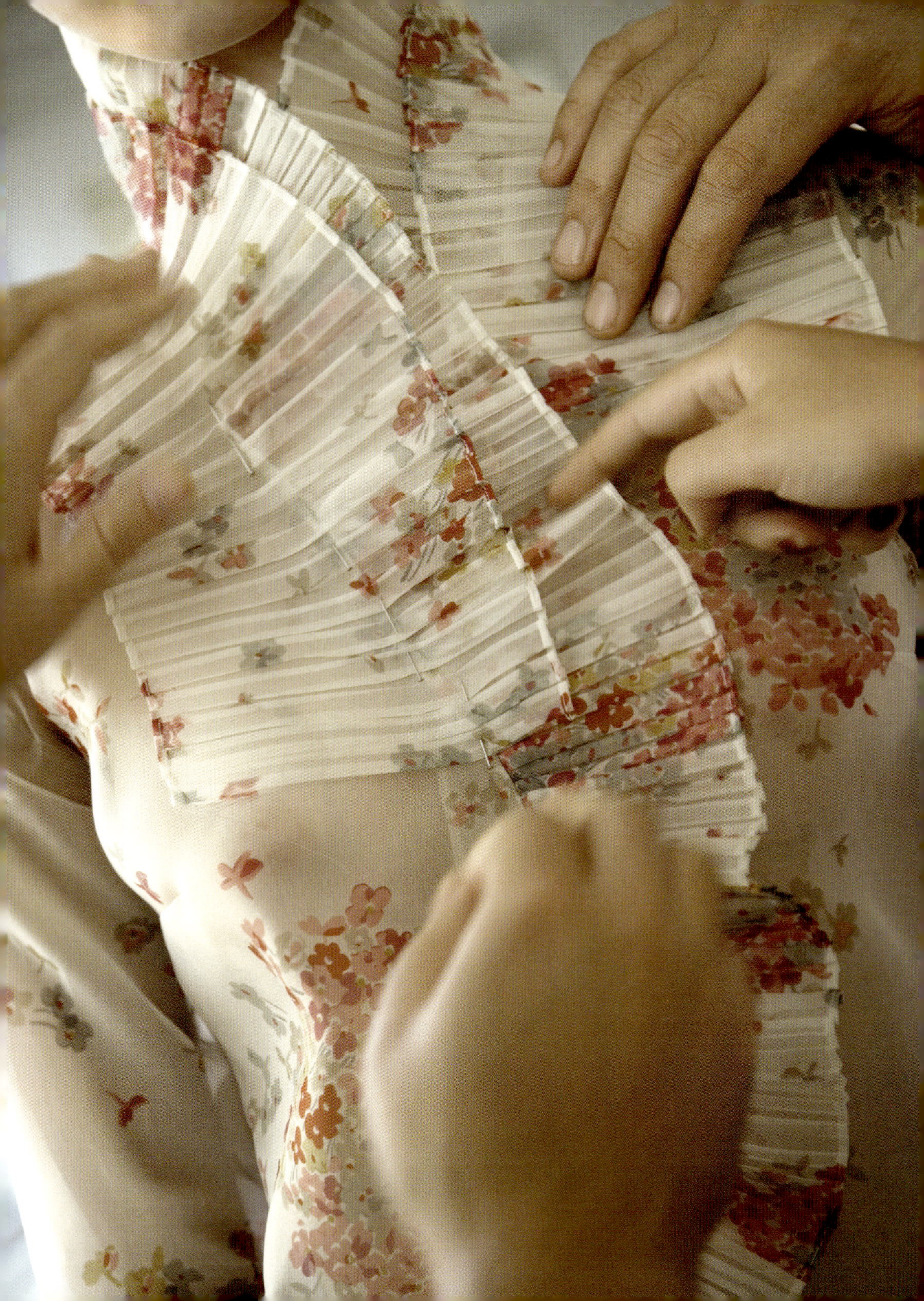

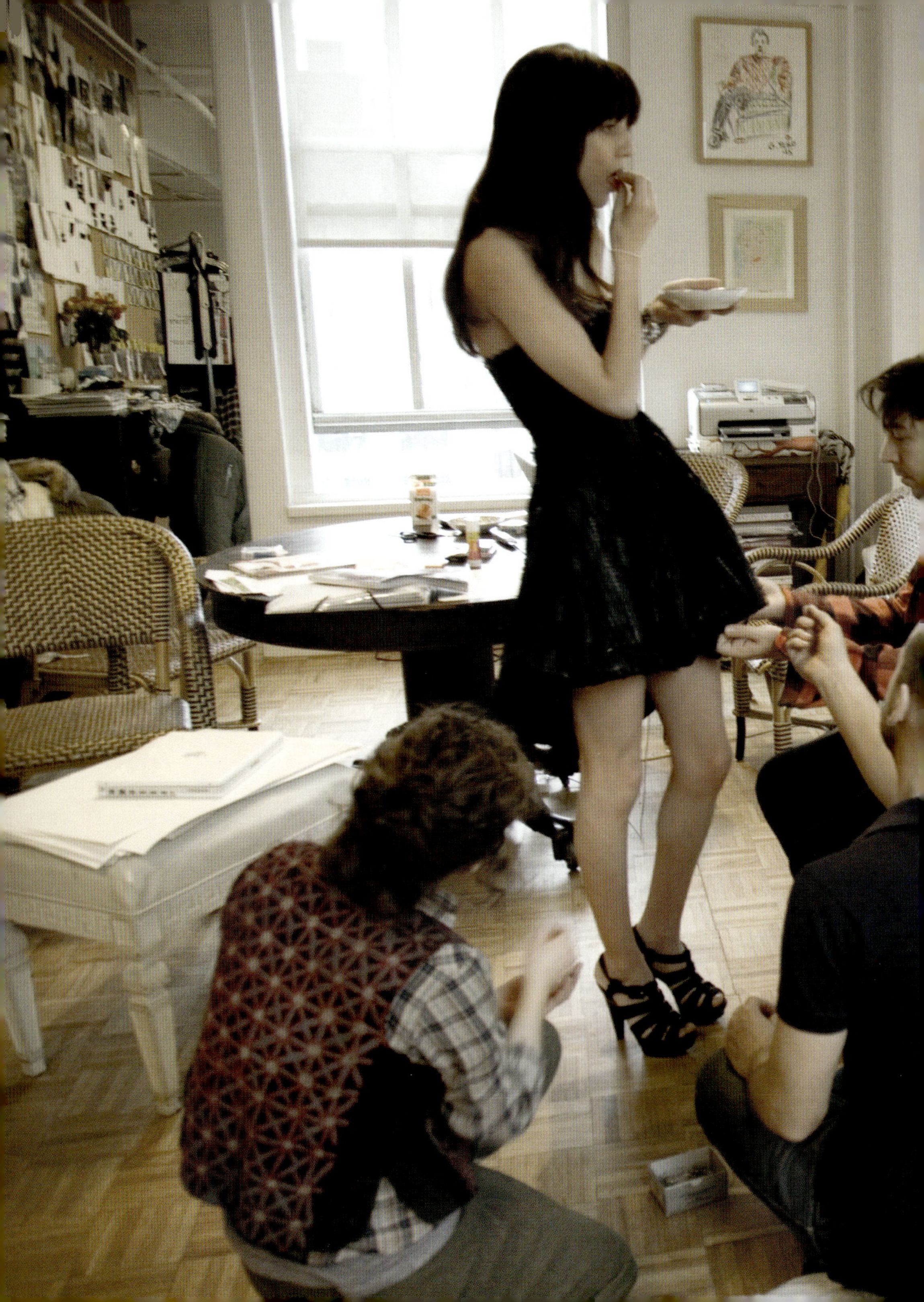

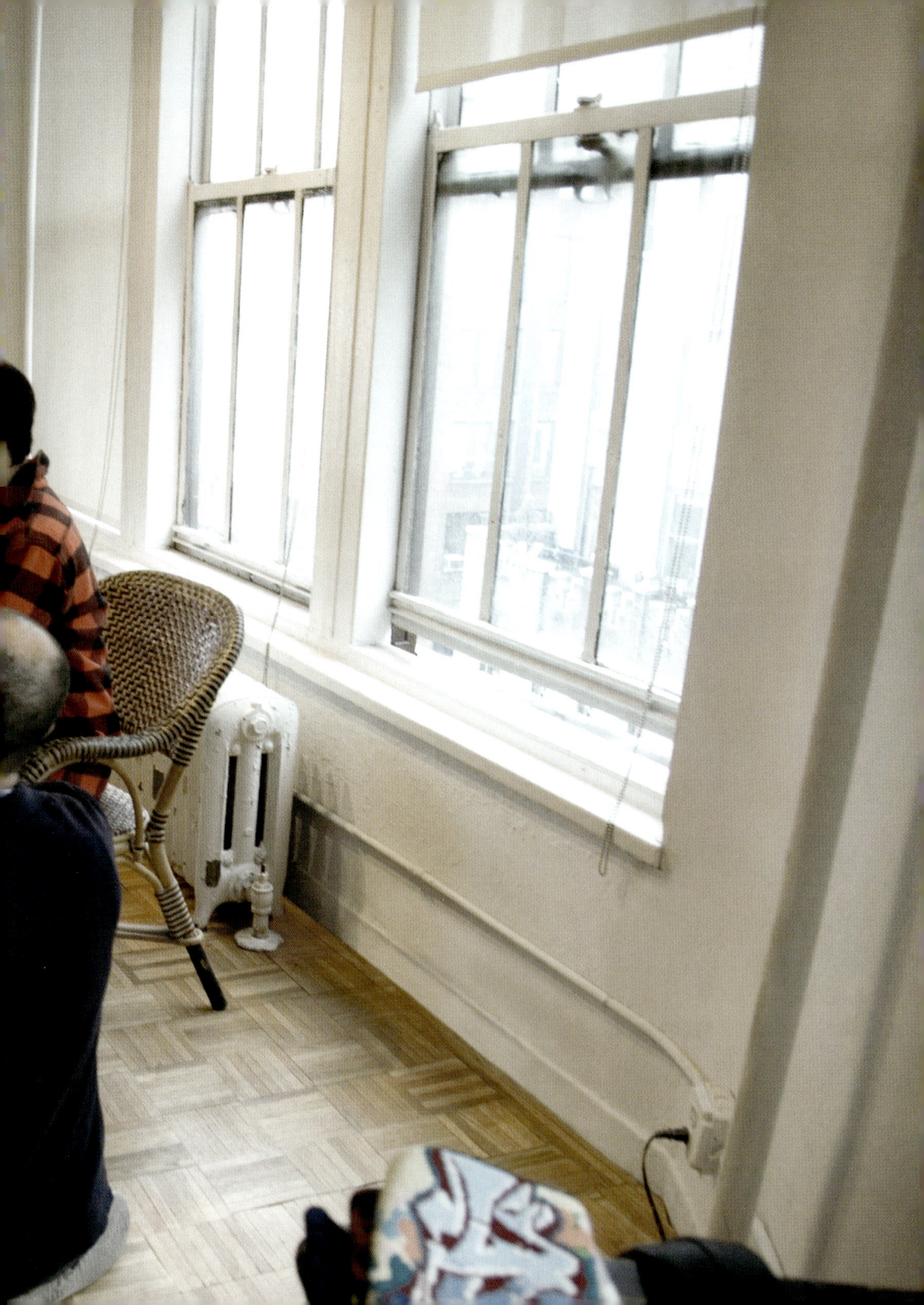

66But today: I return to the studios, especially those of young designers. My favorite of the moment is Ruffian.99

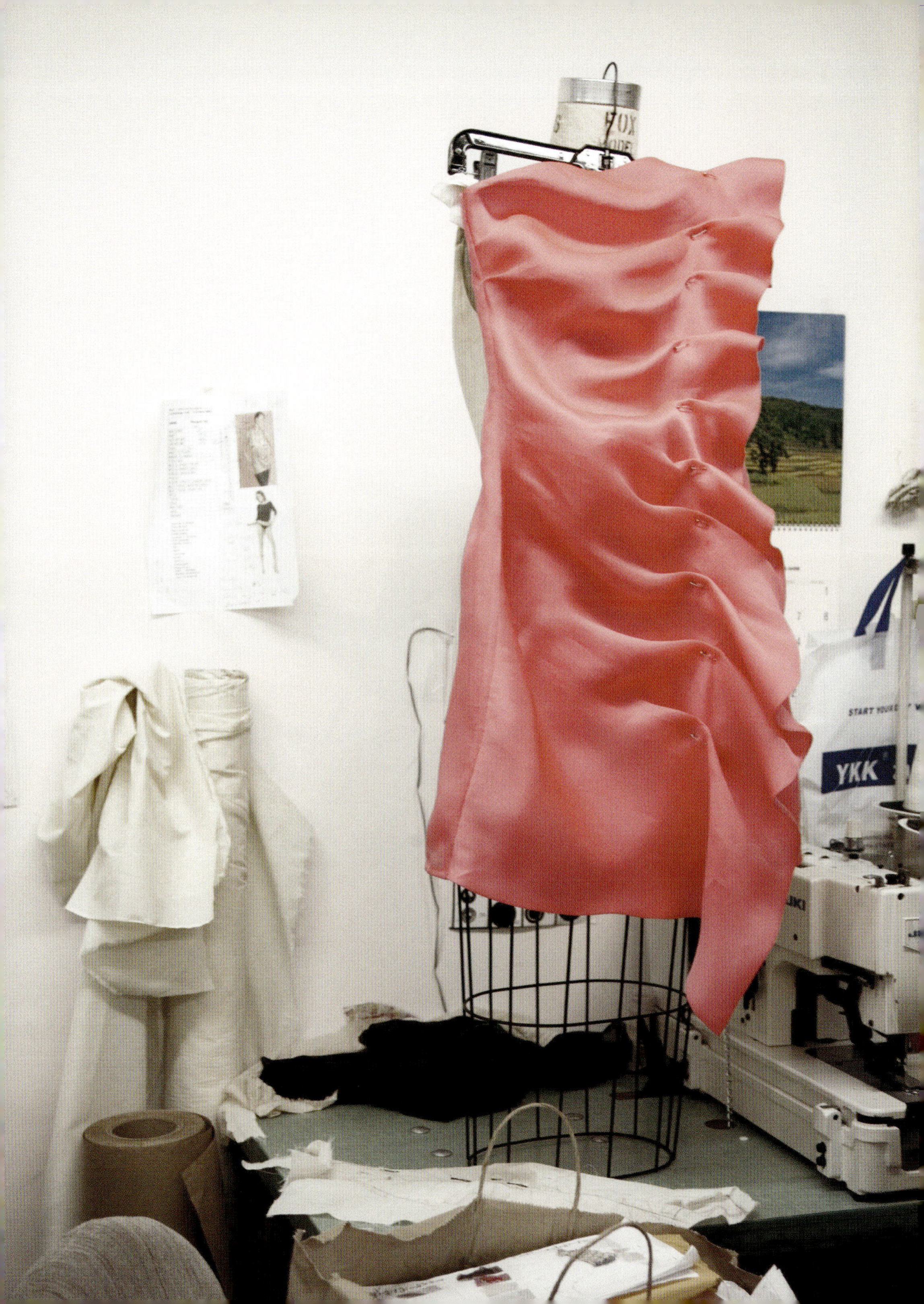

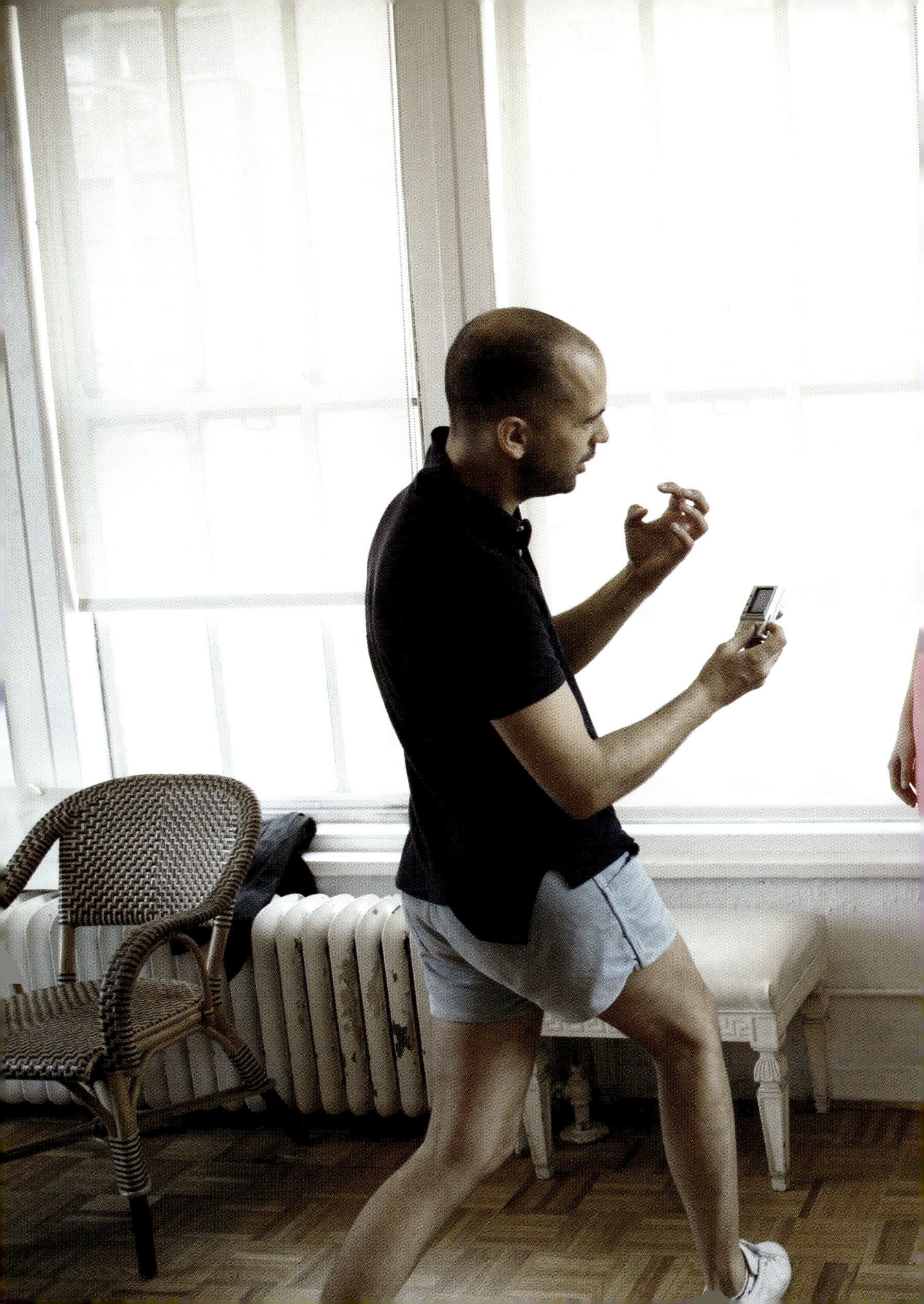

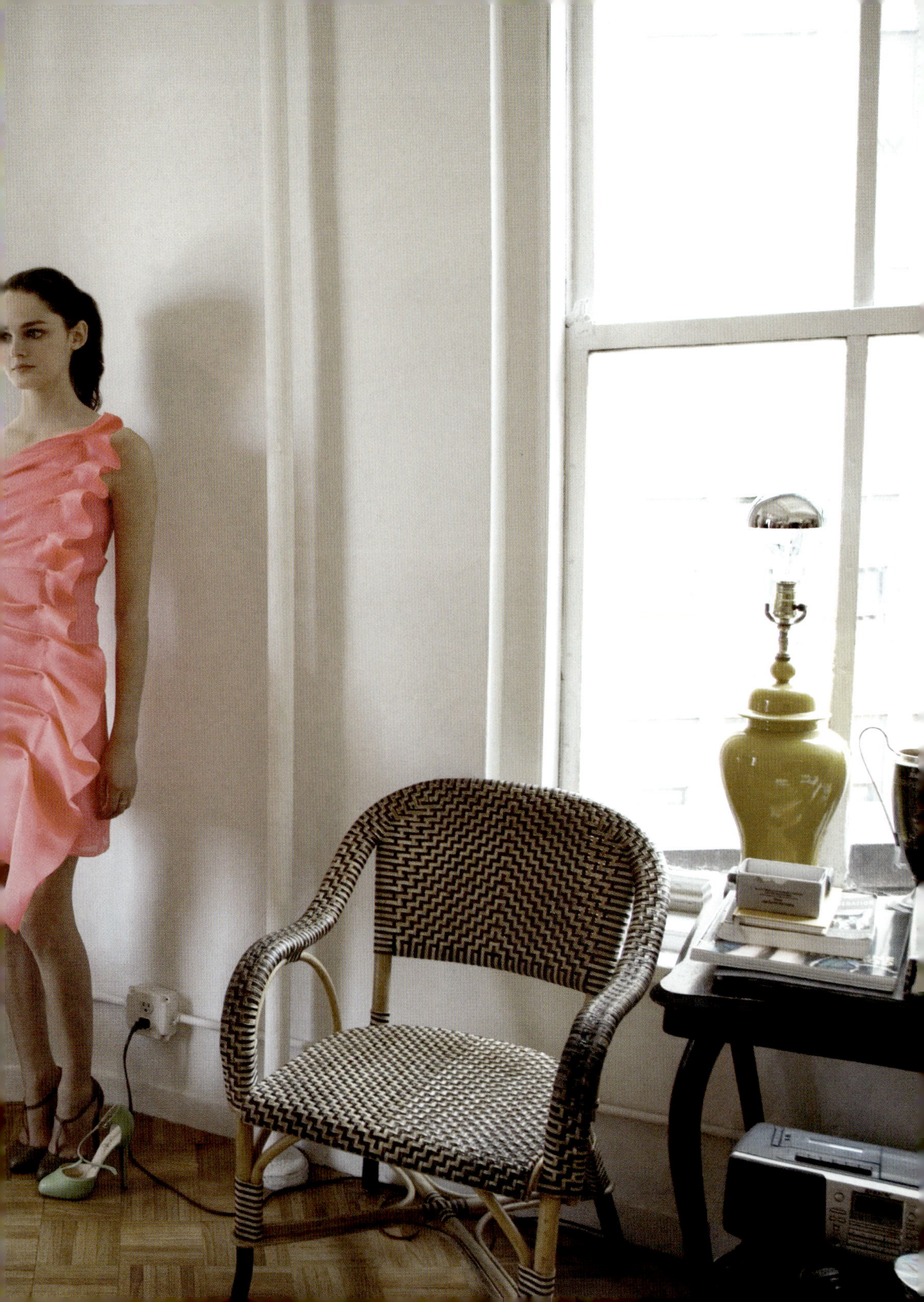

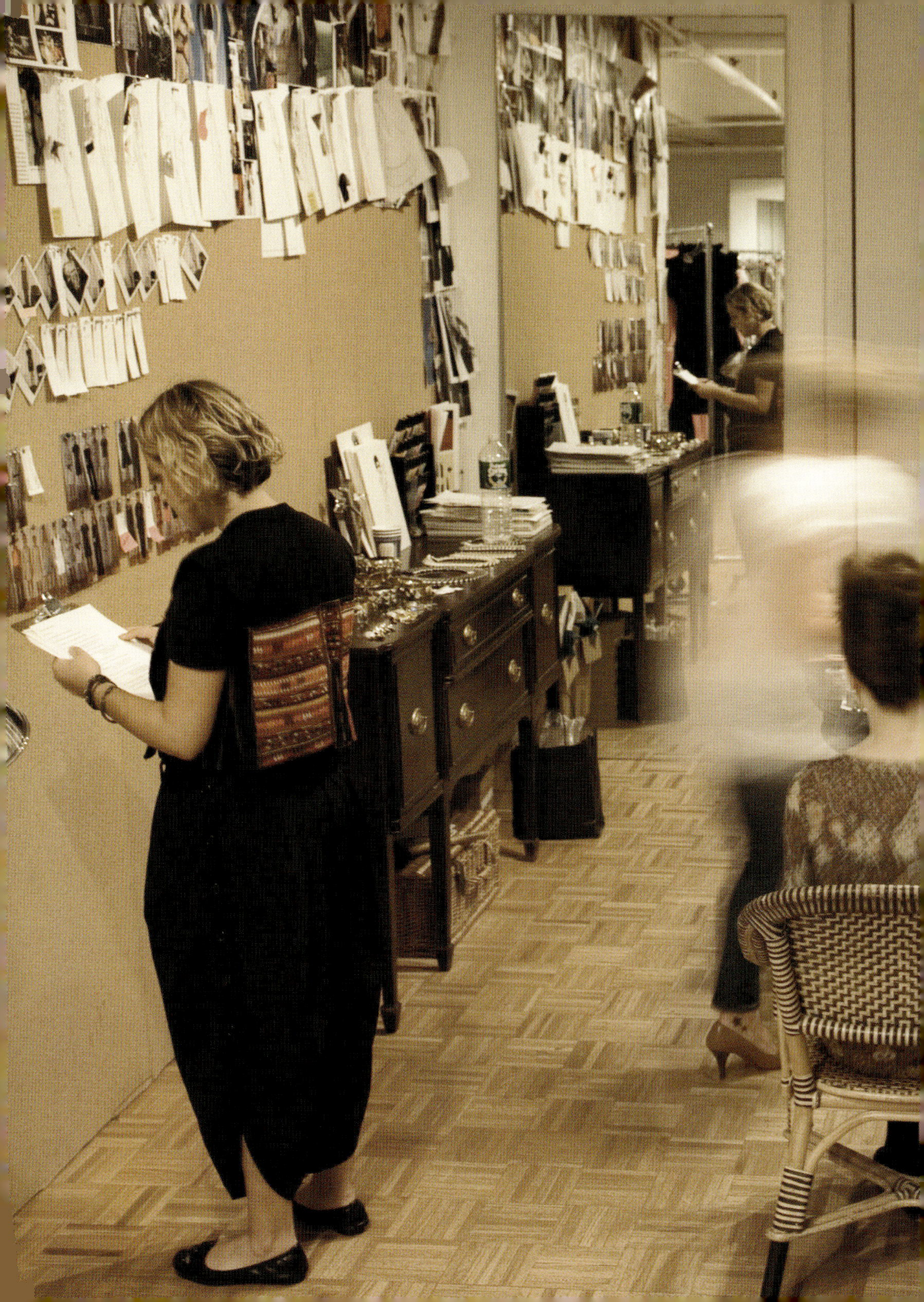

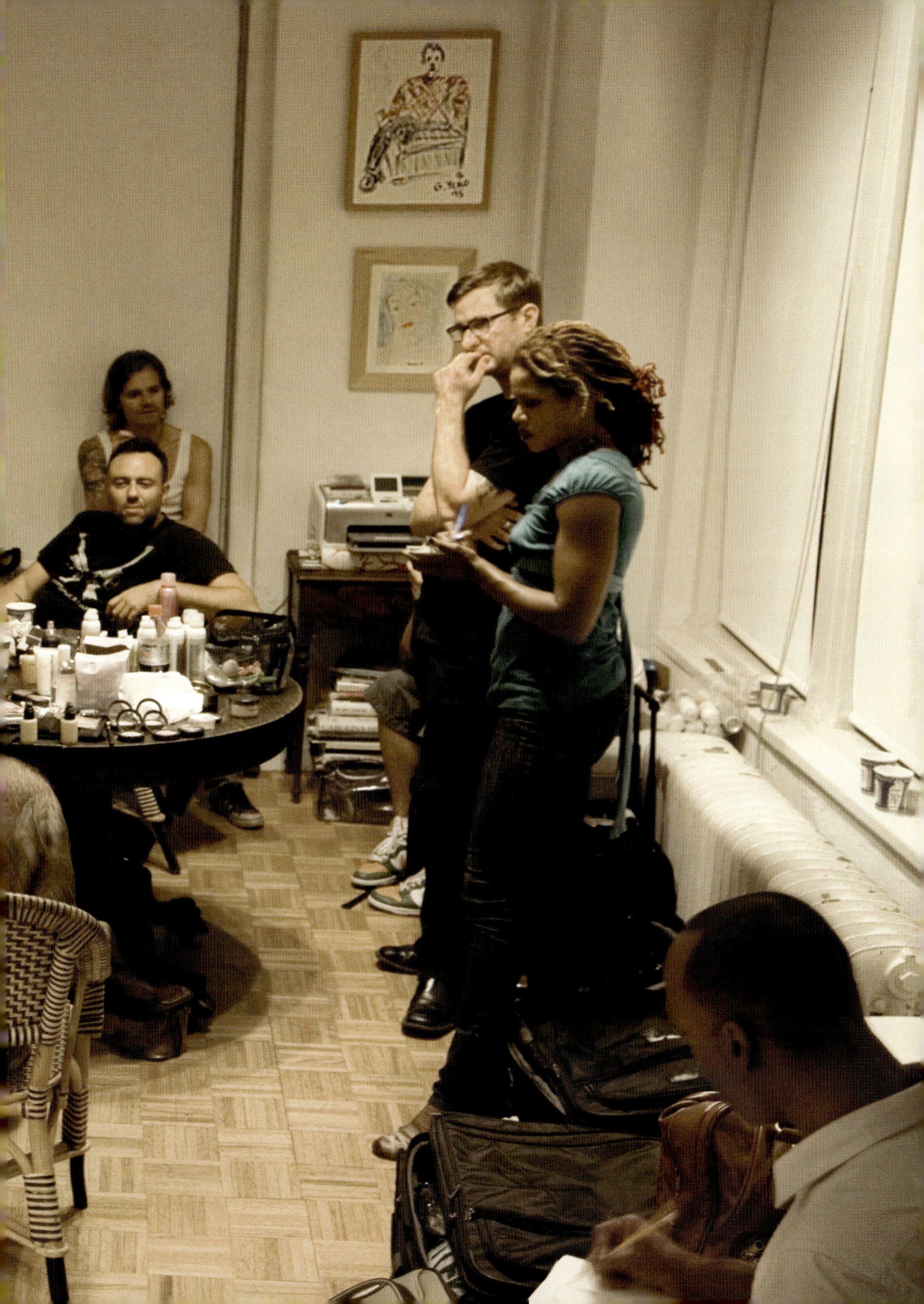

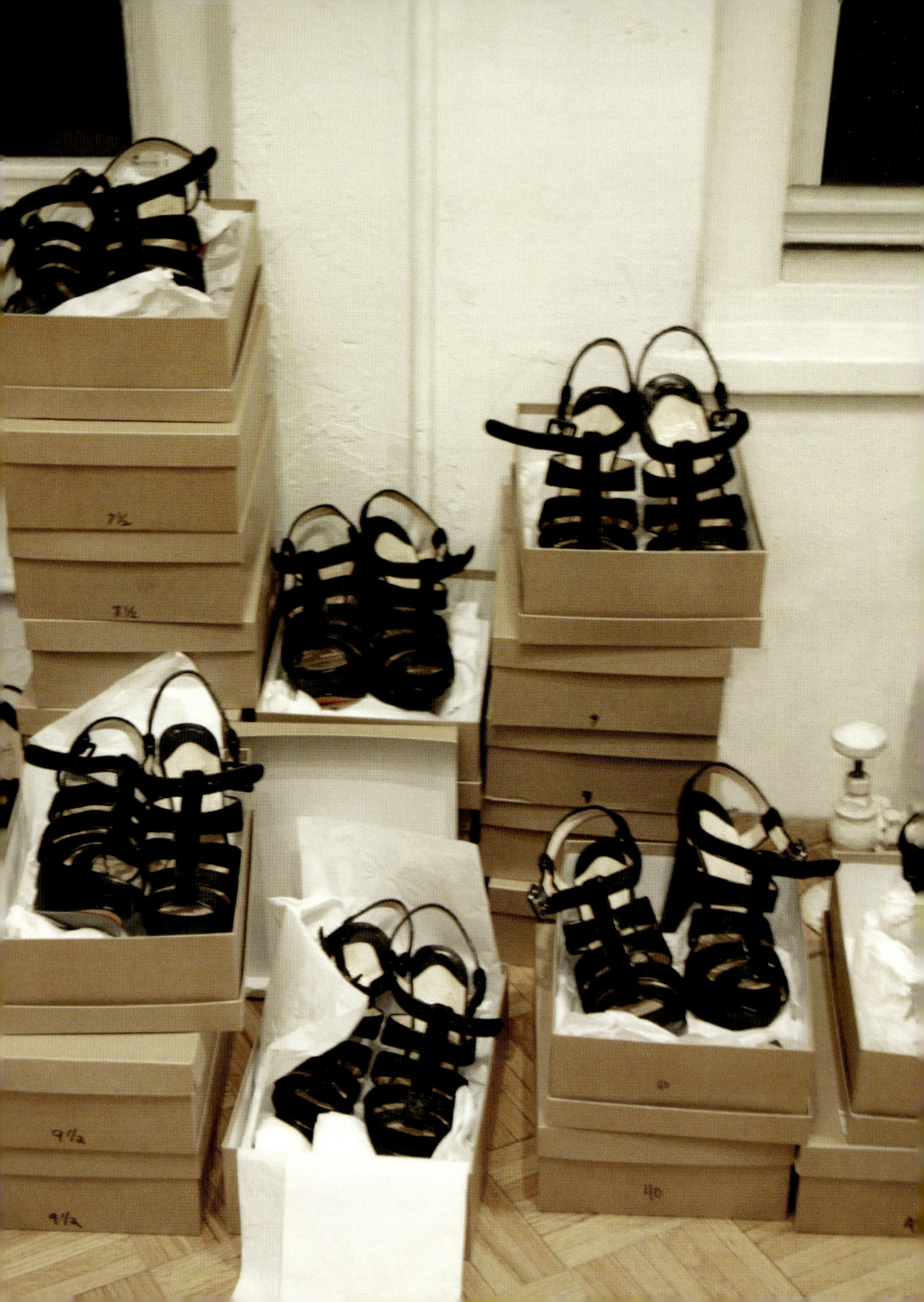

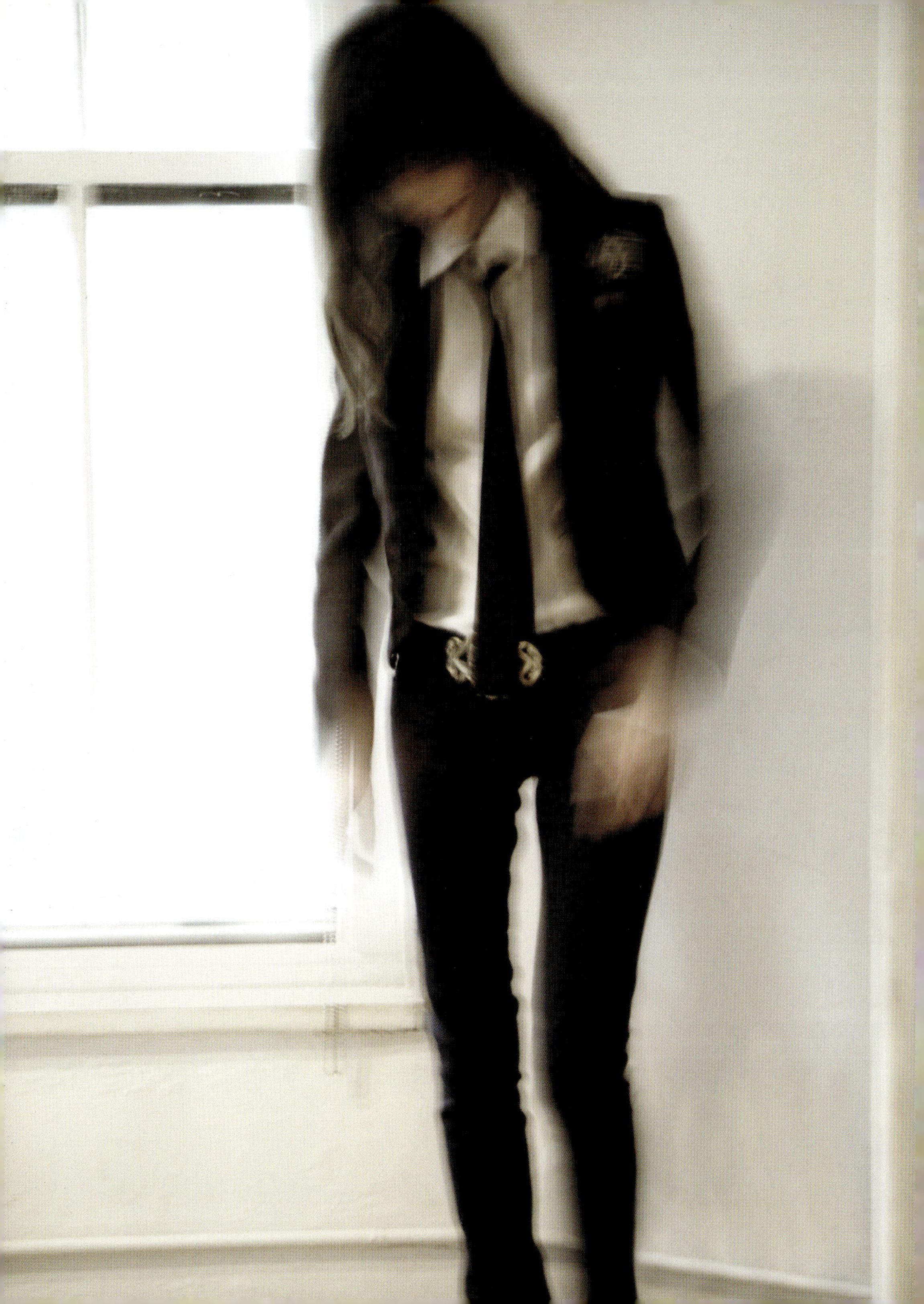

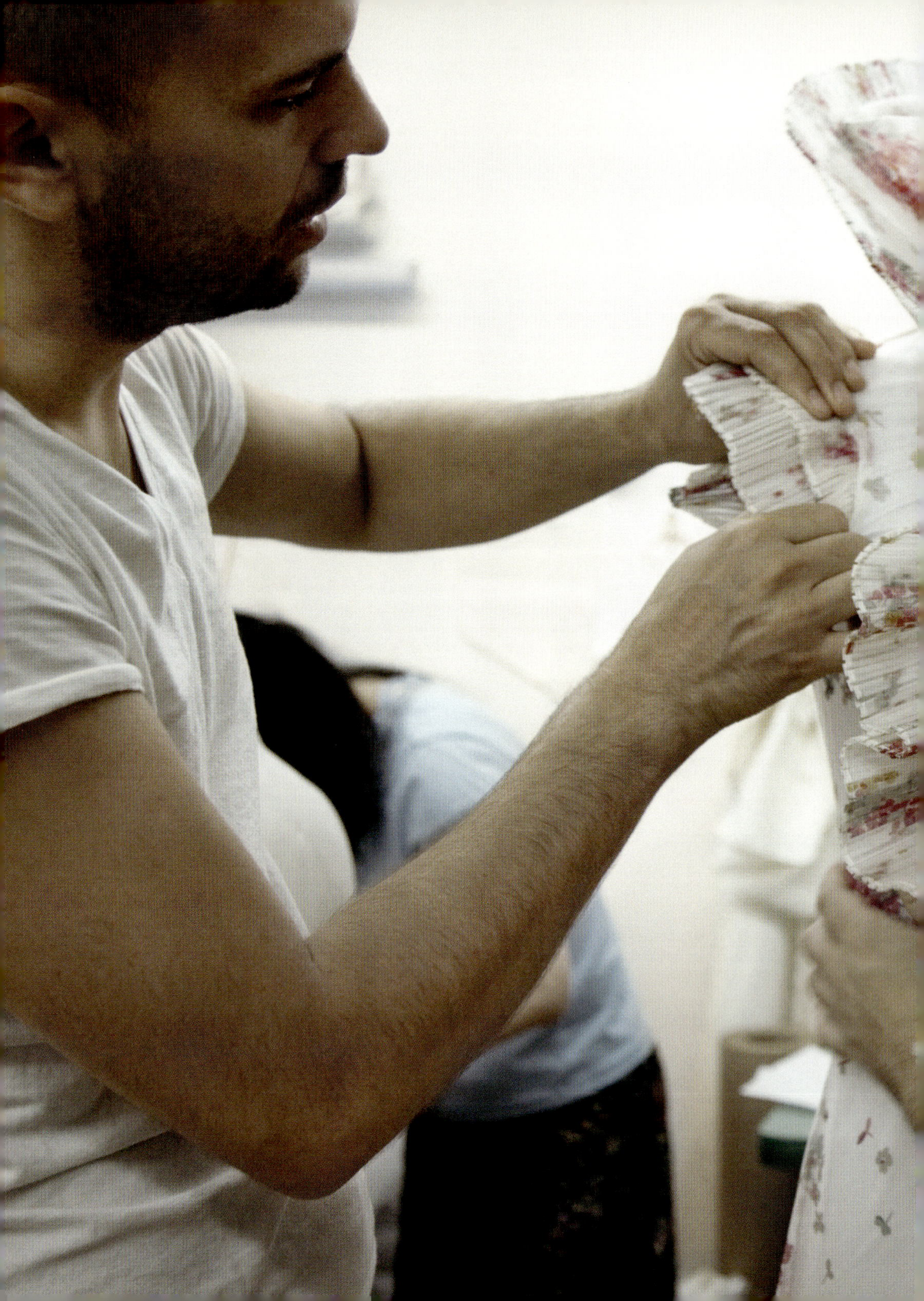

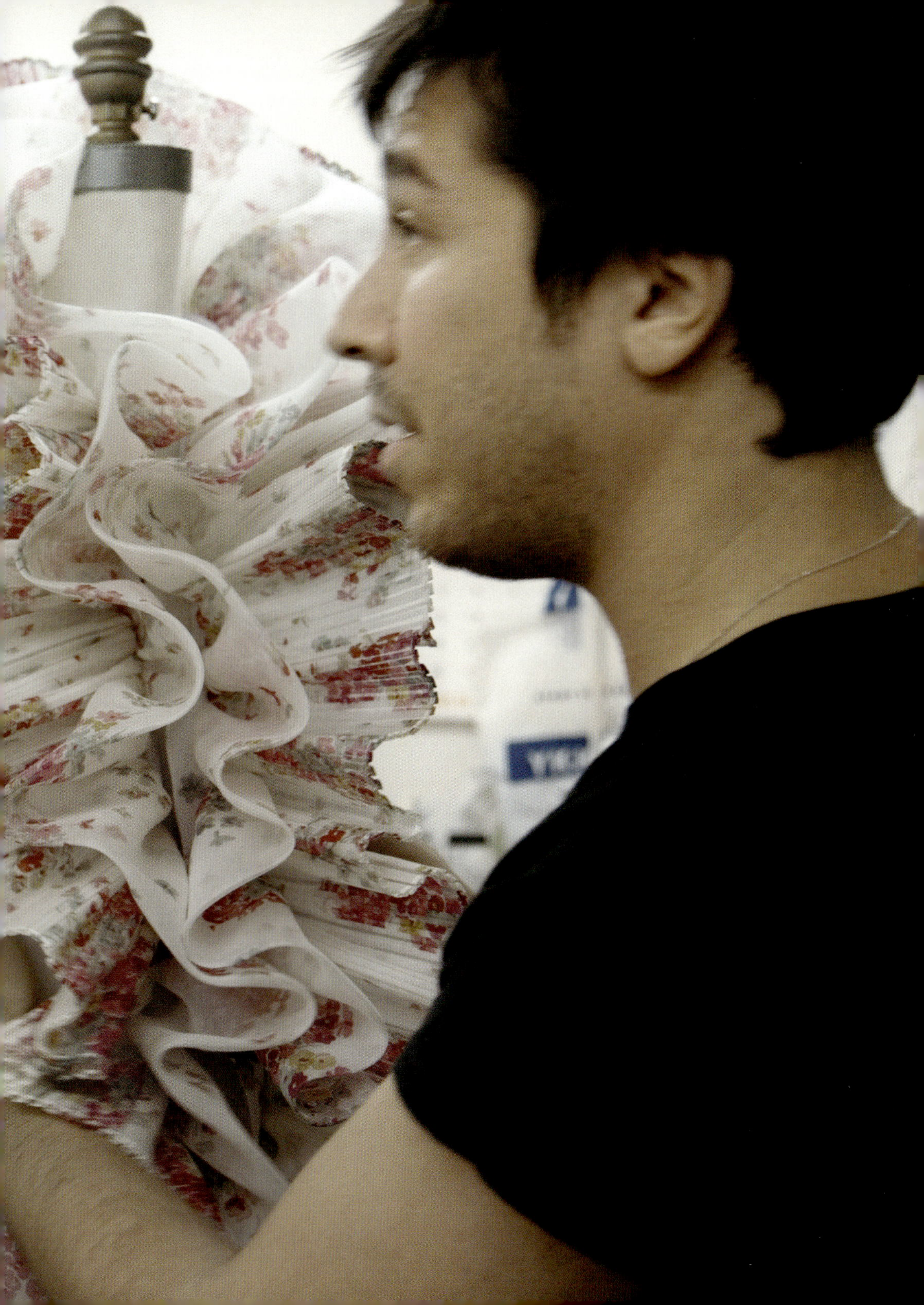

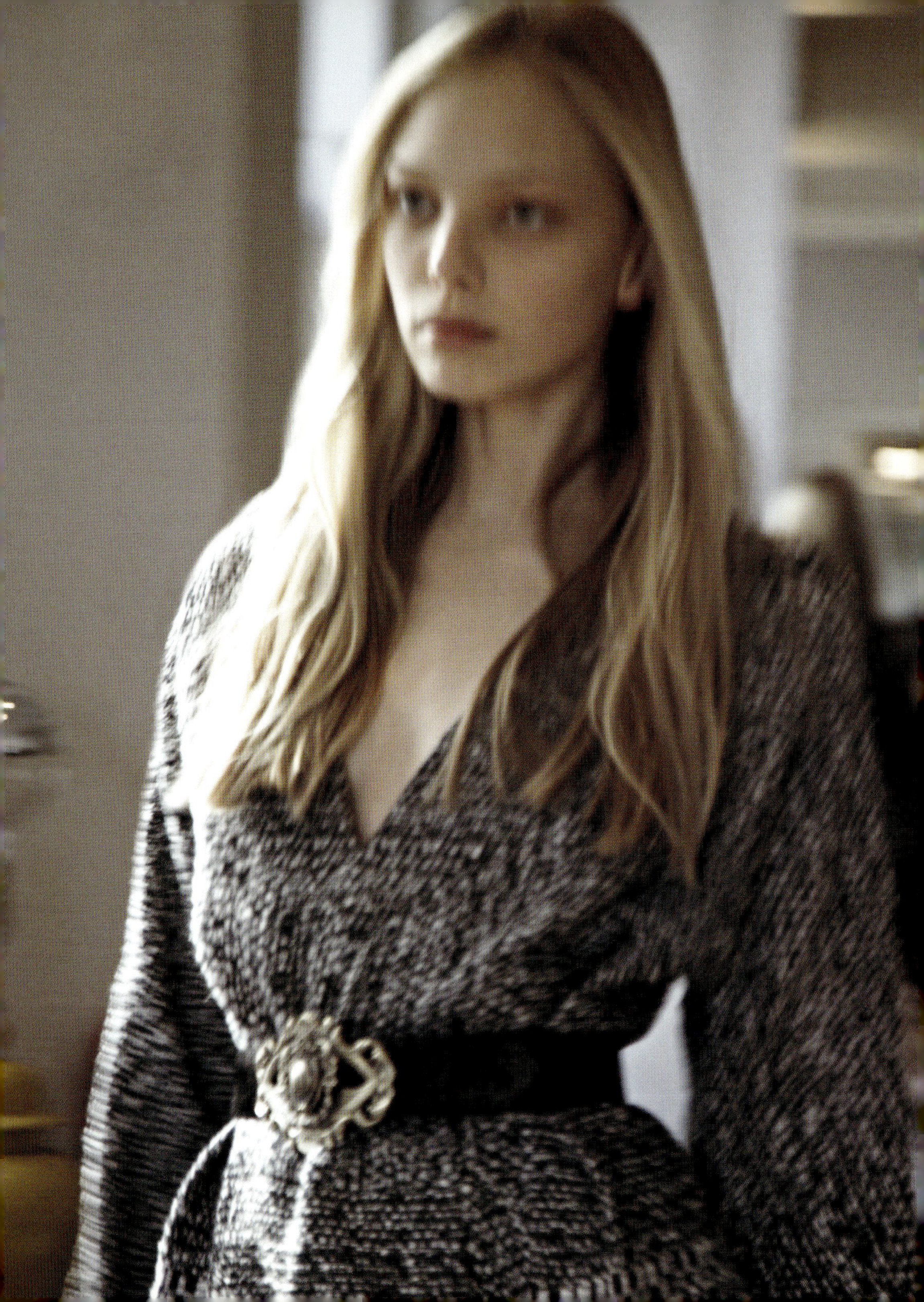

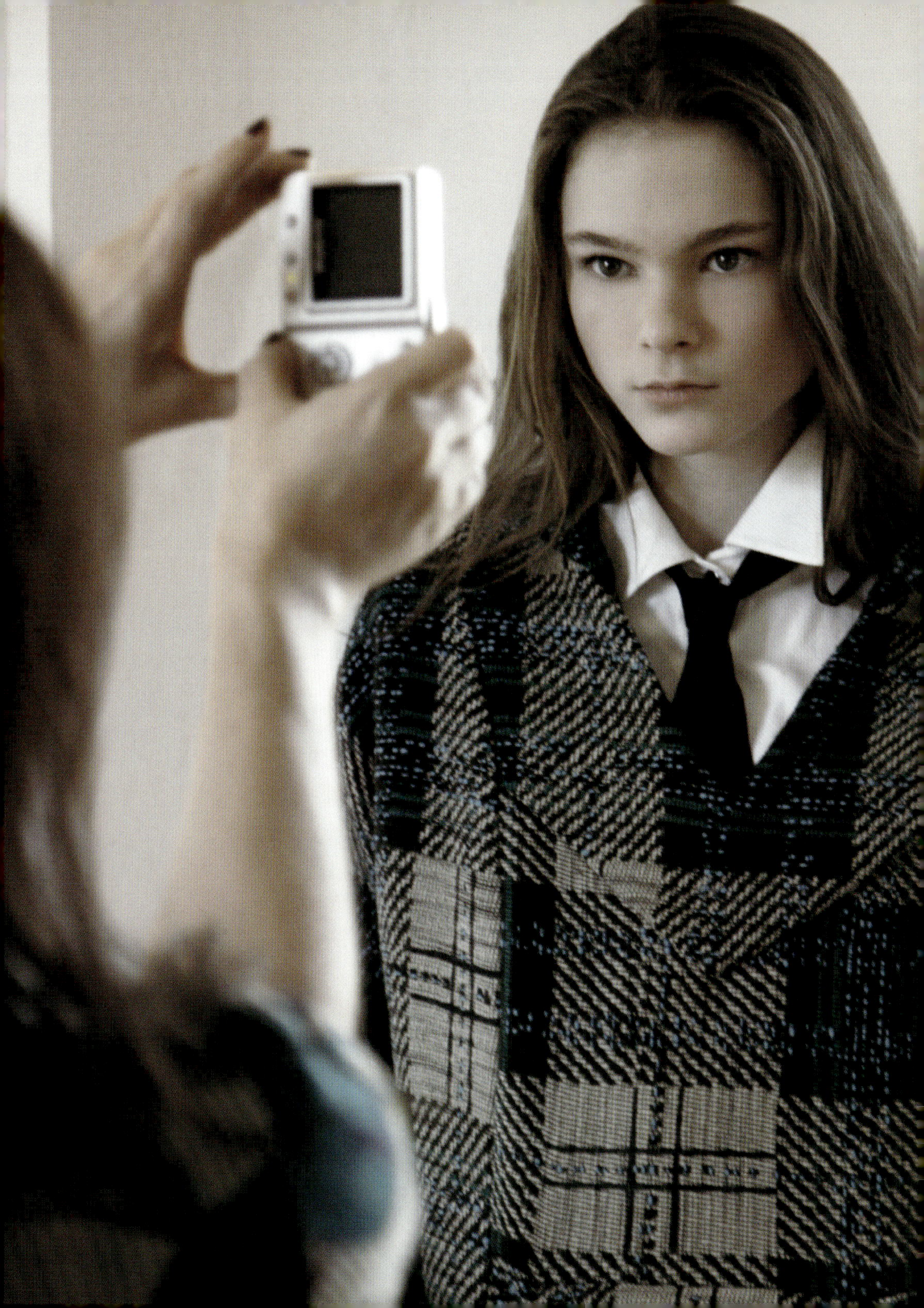

"The boys make deathly beautiful clothes, and continue to define and solidify their aesthetic, which follows this formula: reference something incredibly glamourous, decadent, rip away all the frills and pretension; inject a whimsical new-wave/post-punk sensibility."

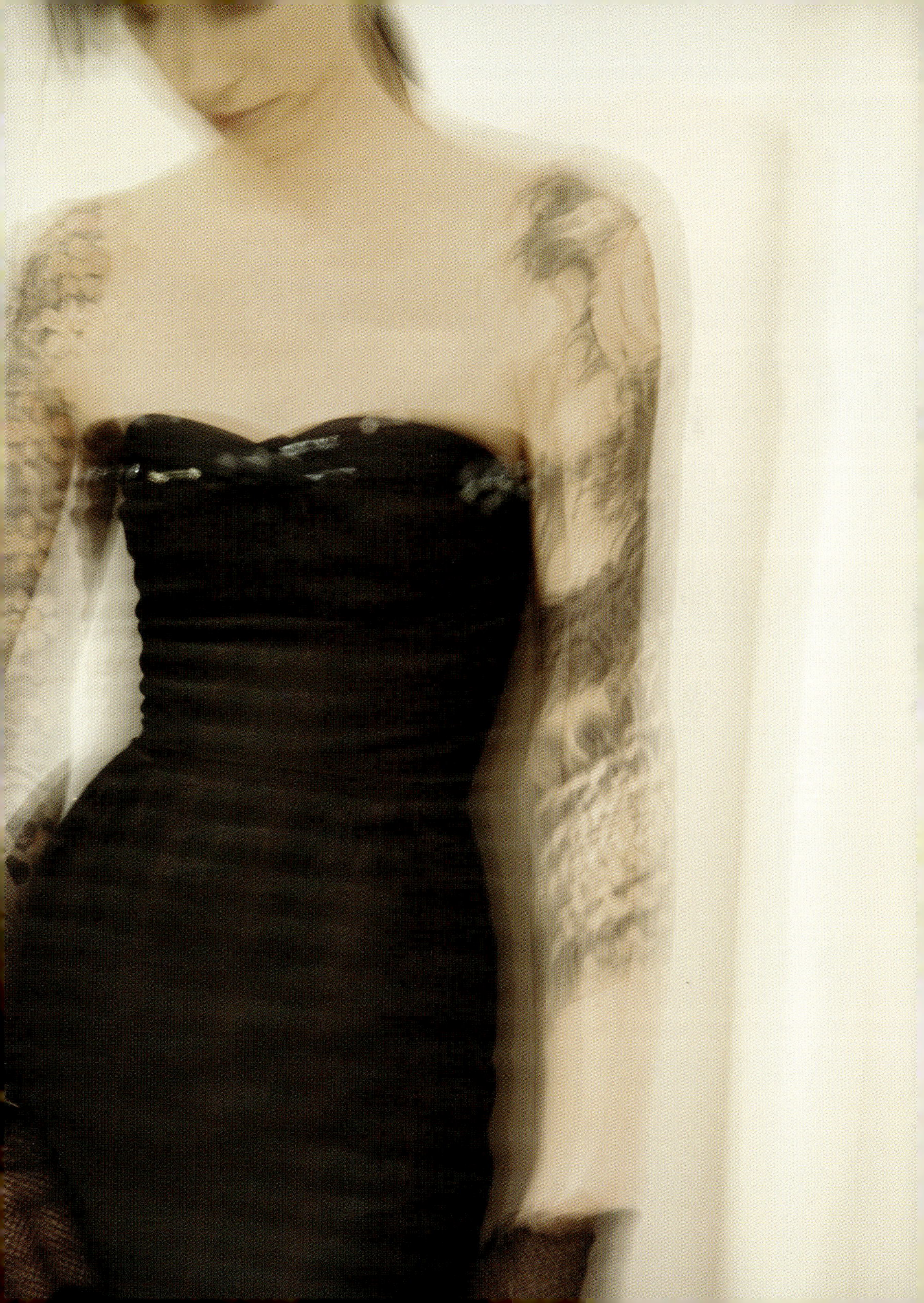

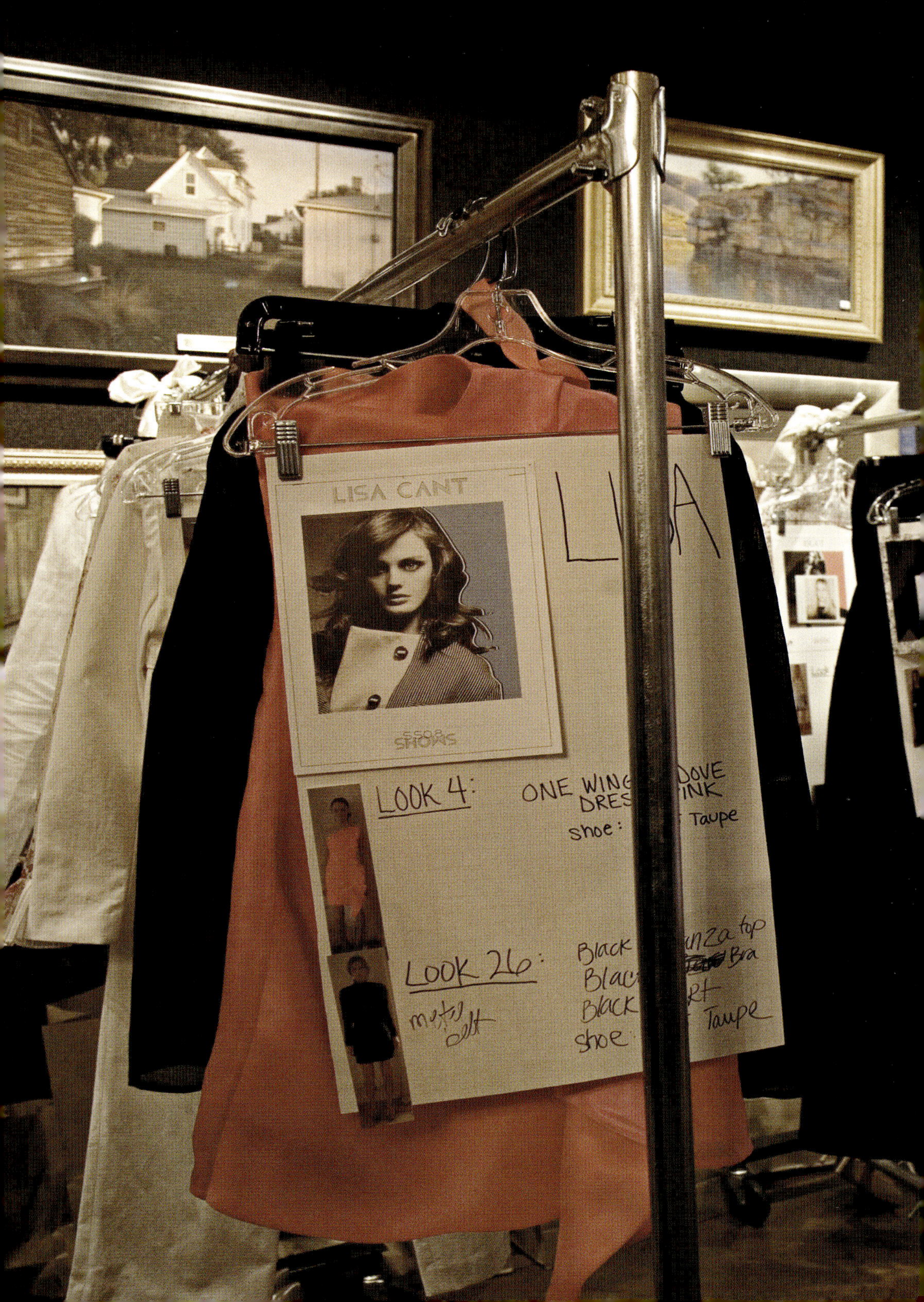

LISA CANT
LISA
SHOWS
LOOK 4: ONE WINGED DOVE
DRESS PINK
shoe: Taupe
LOOK 26: Black Organza top
Black Bra
Black skirt
shoe: Taupe

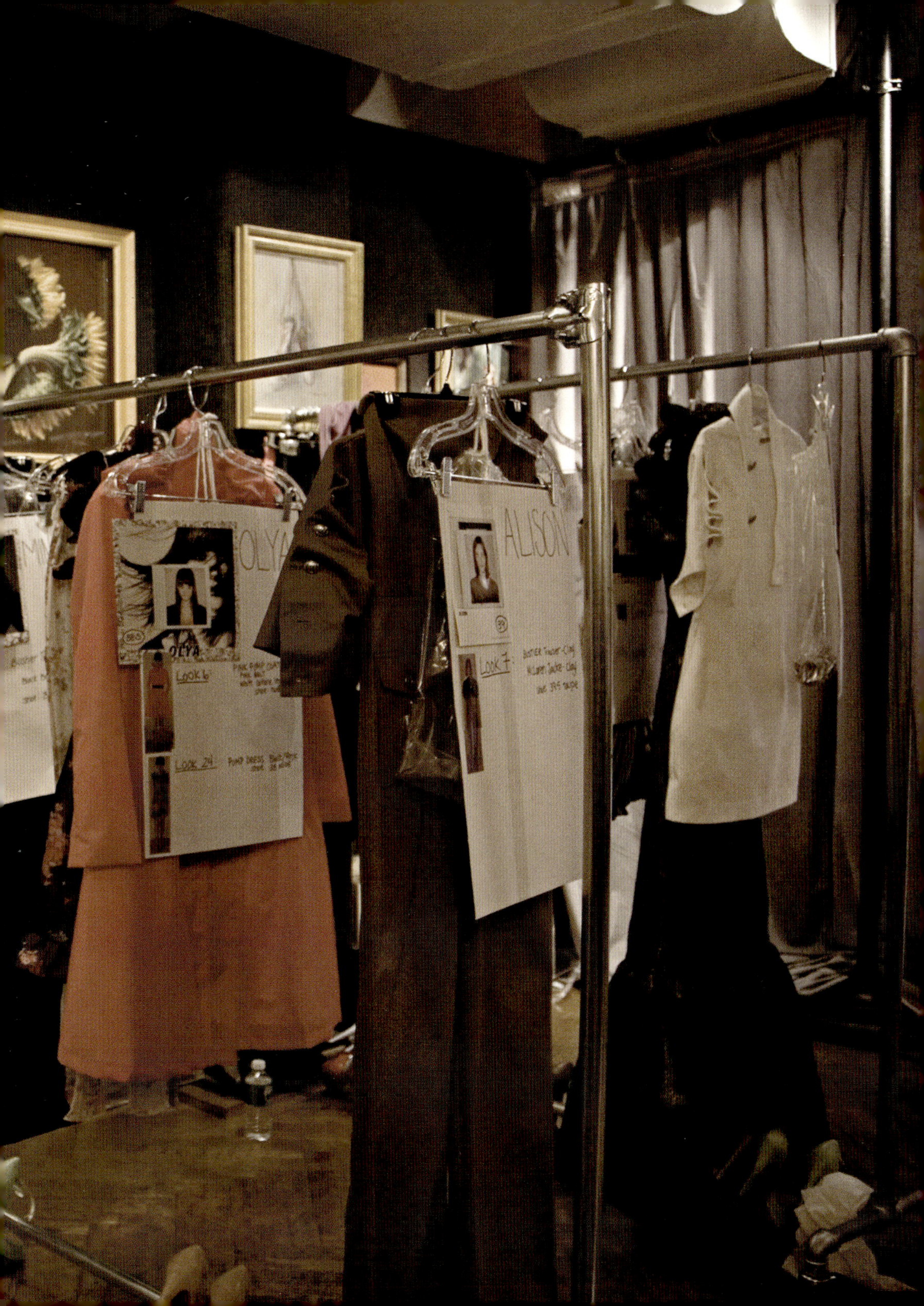

OLYA
OLYA
Look 6
Look 24
ALISON
Look 7

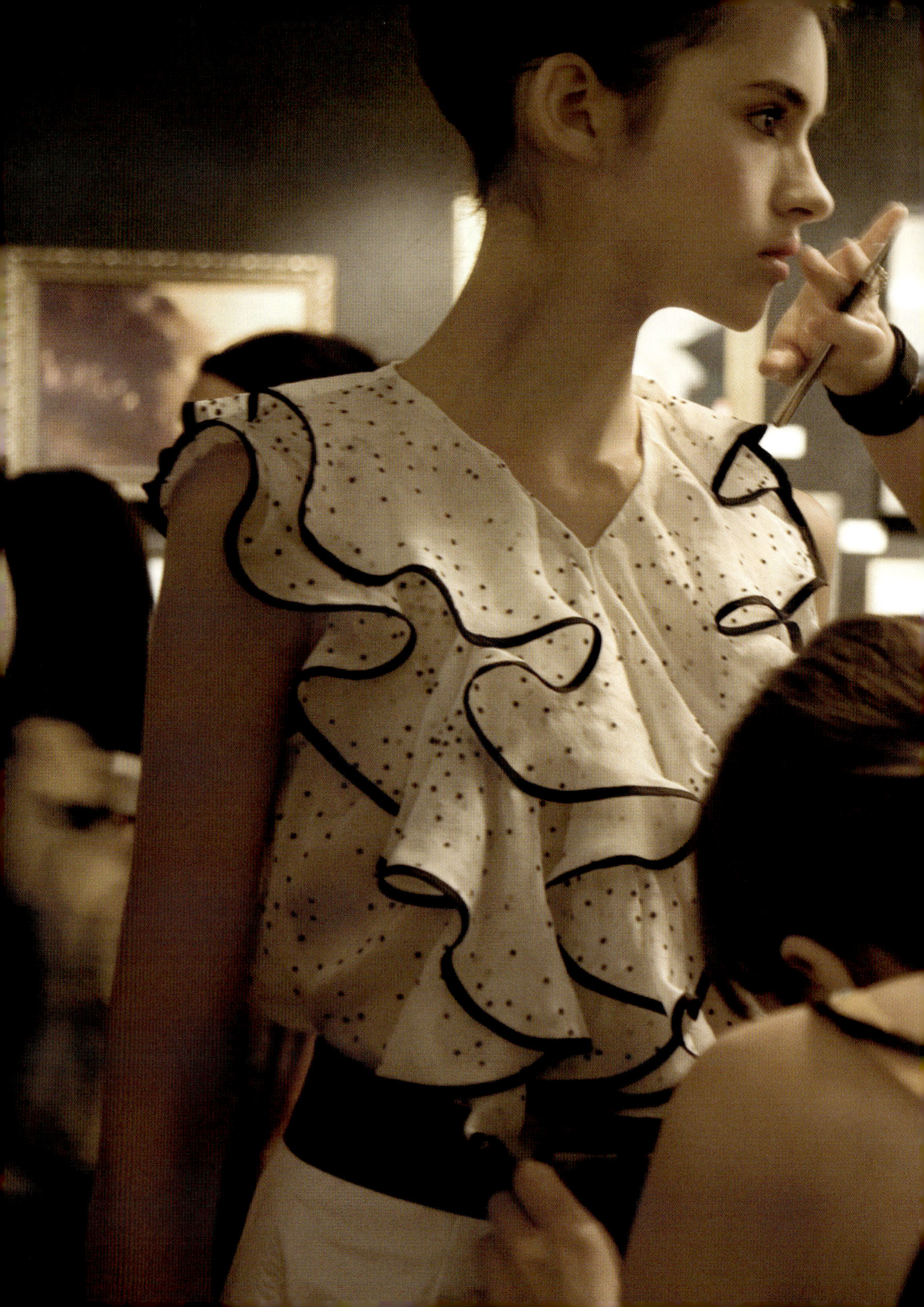

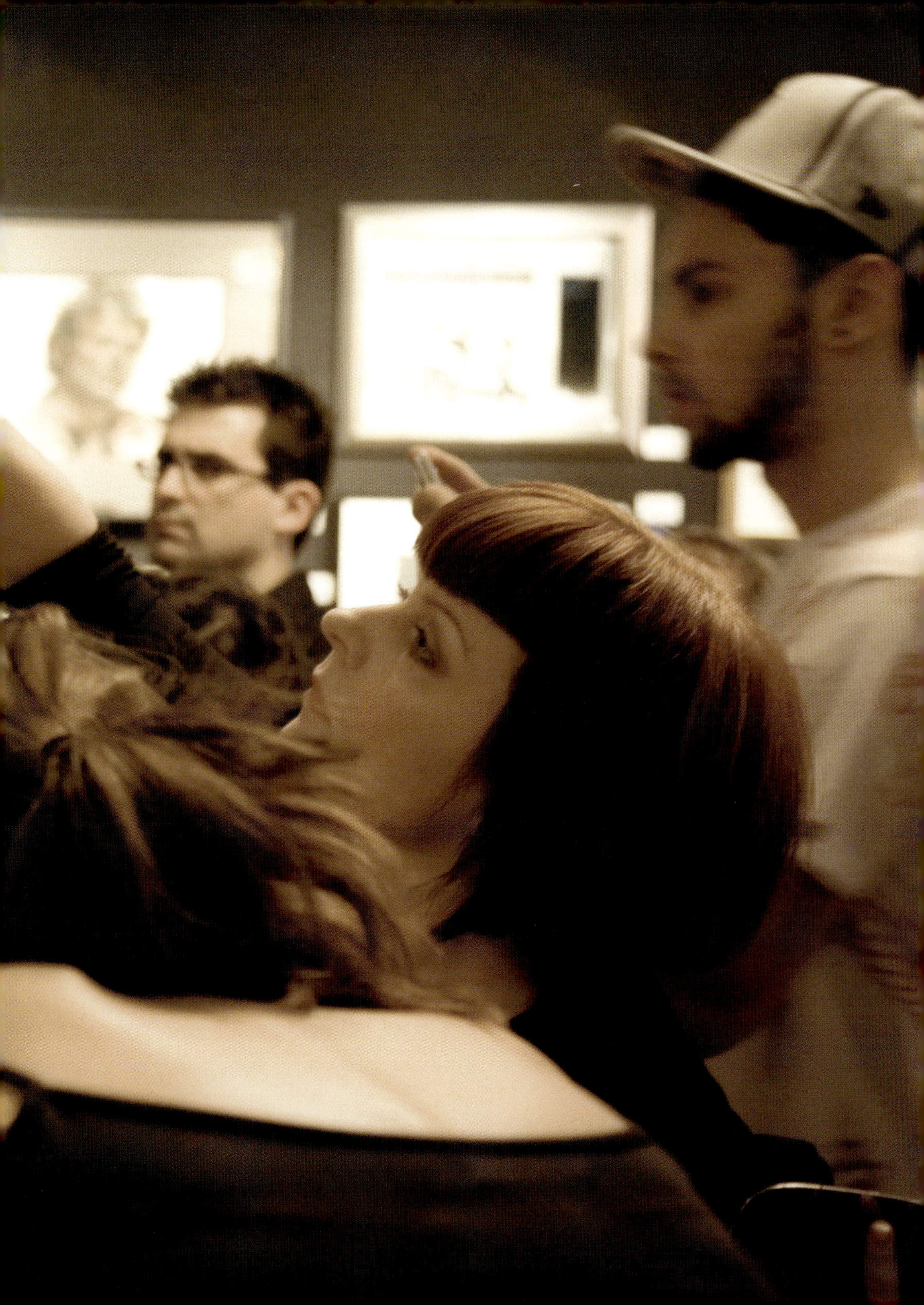

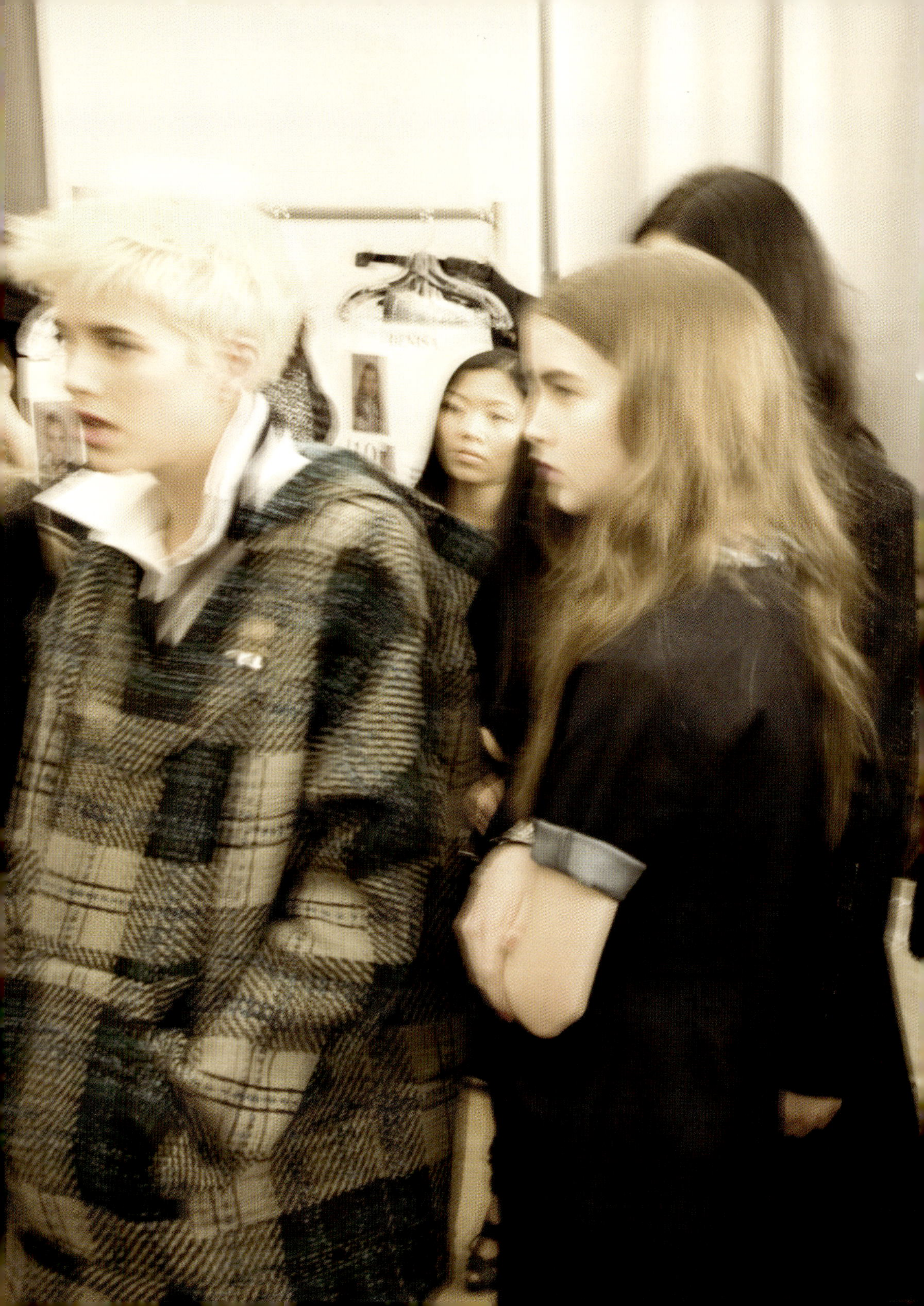

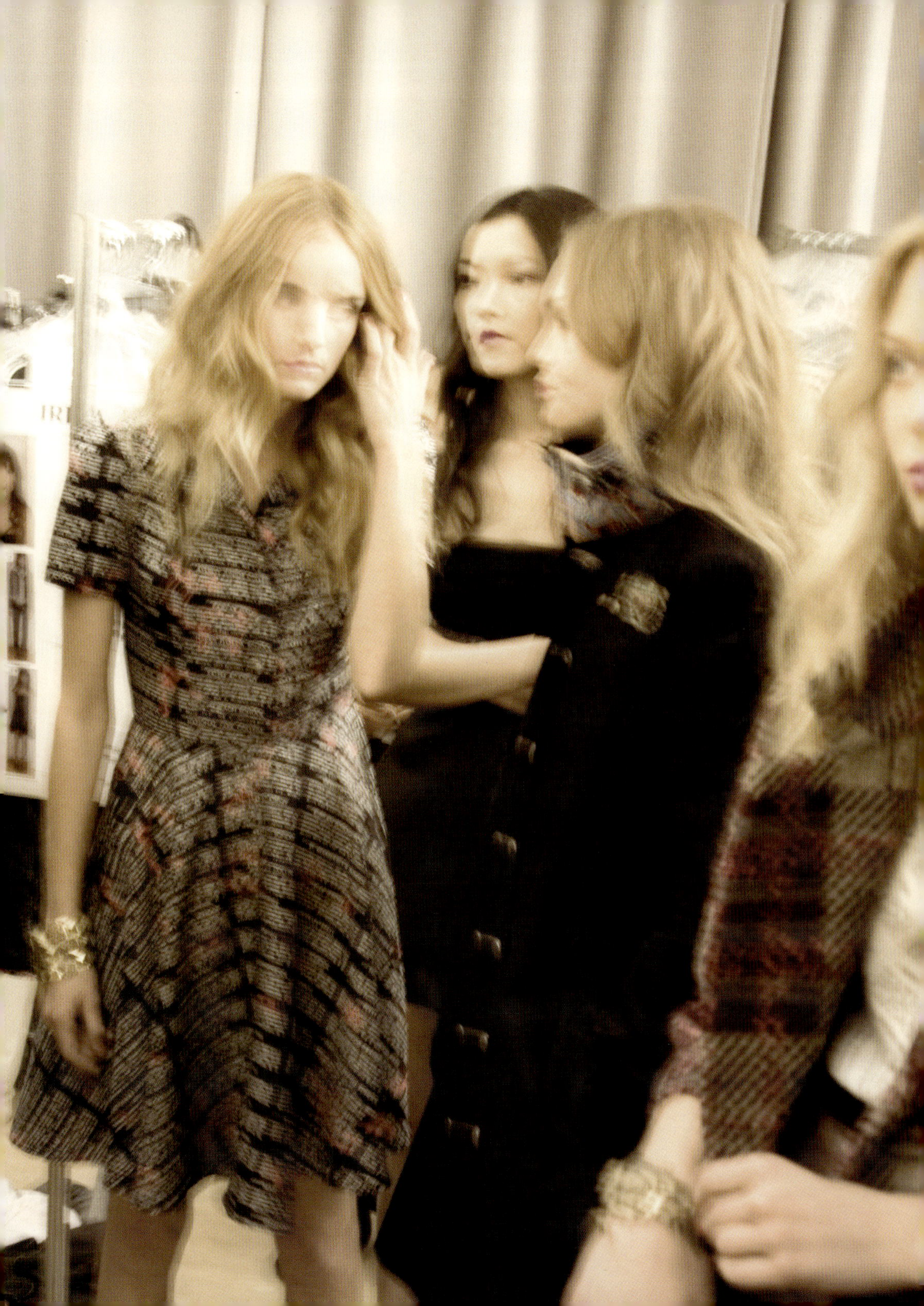

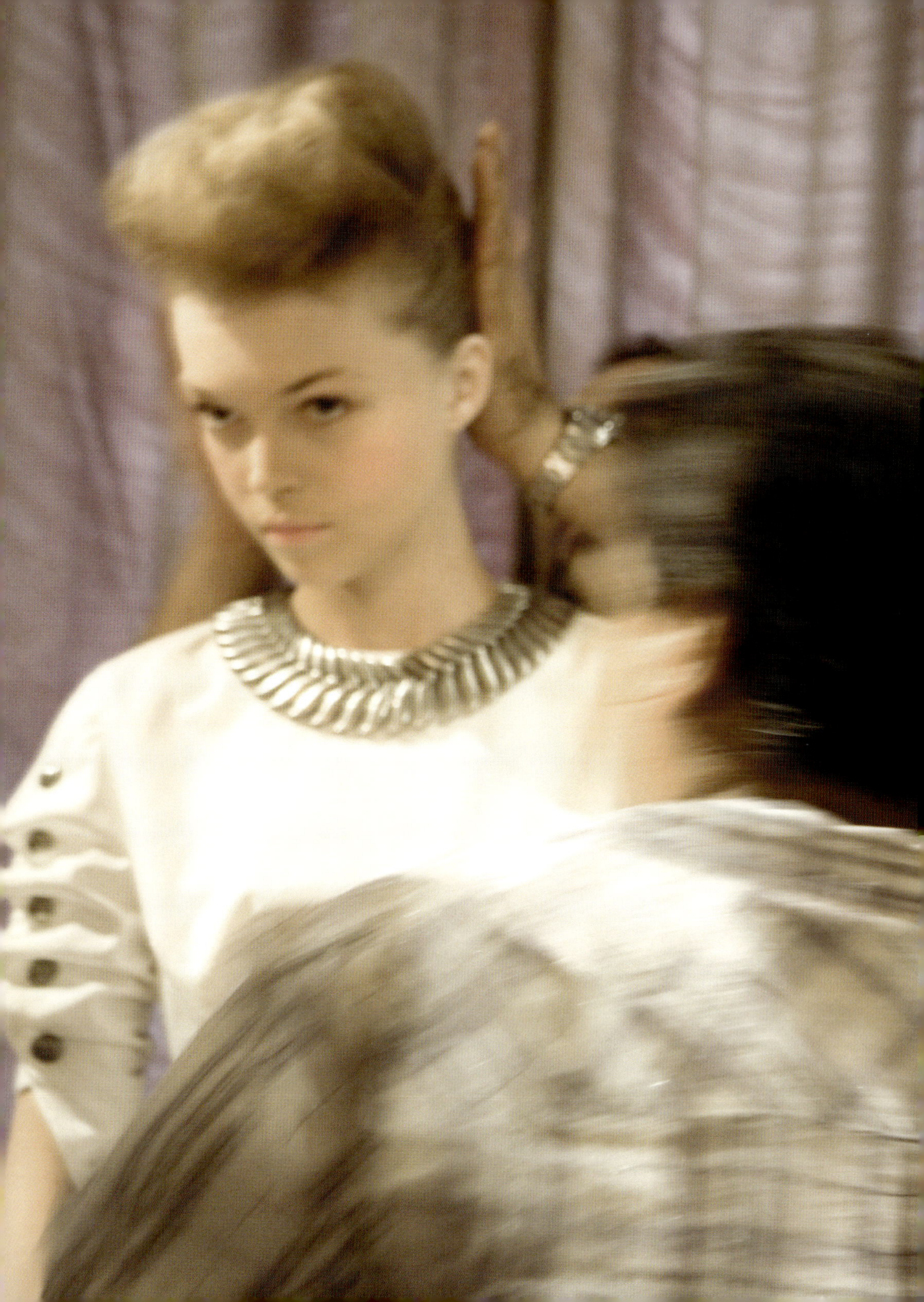

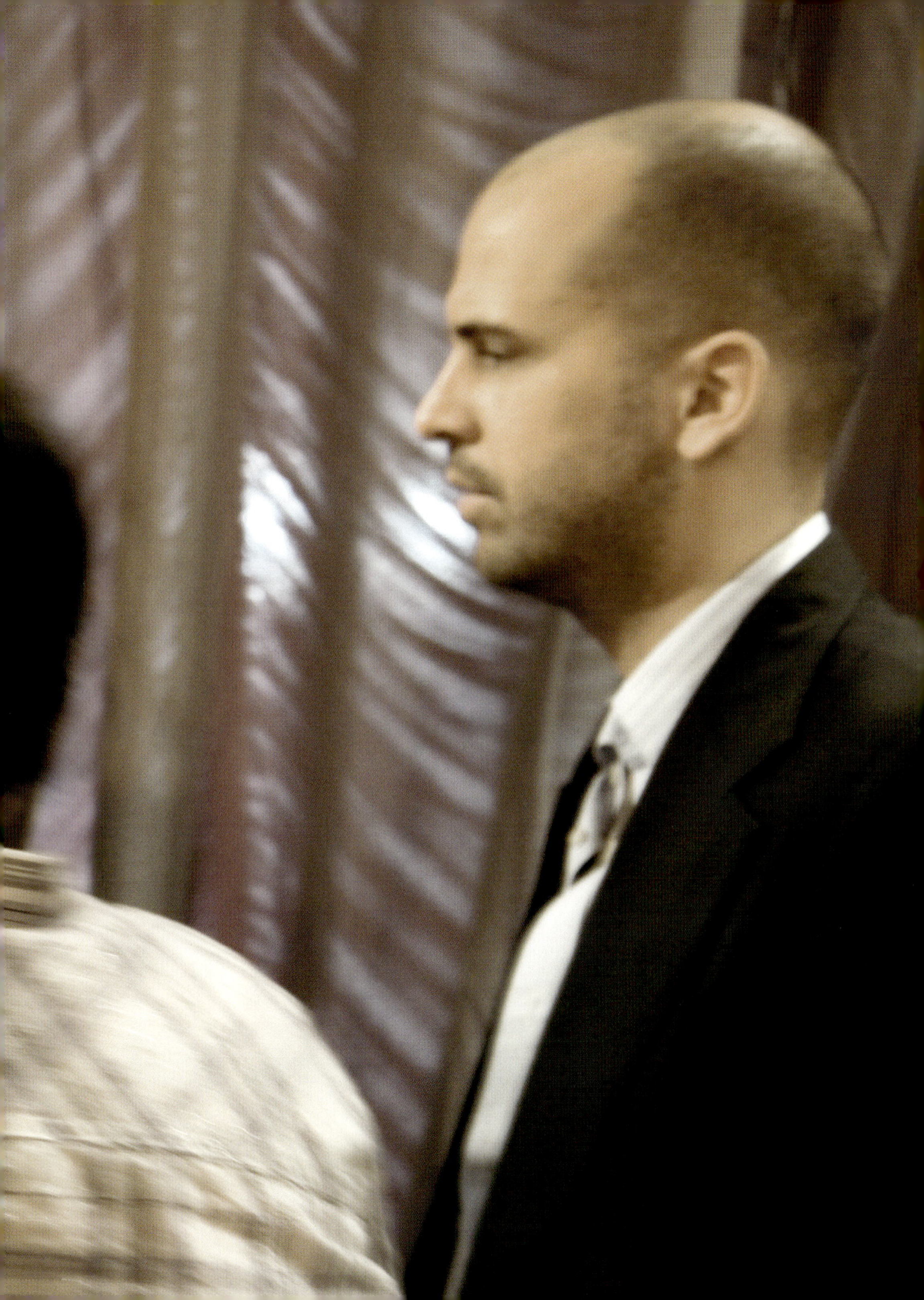

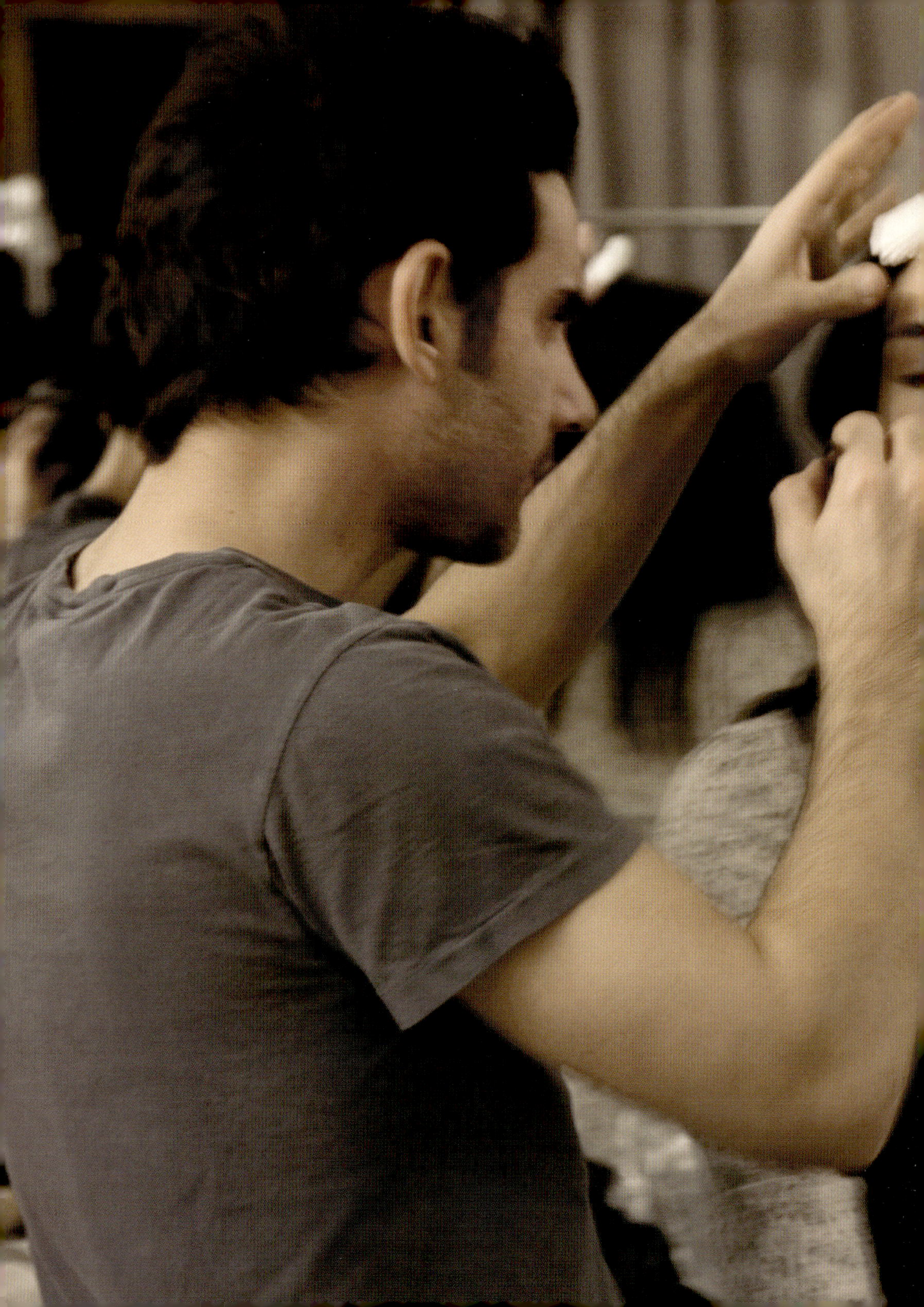

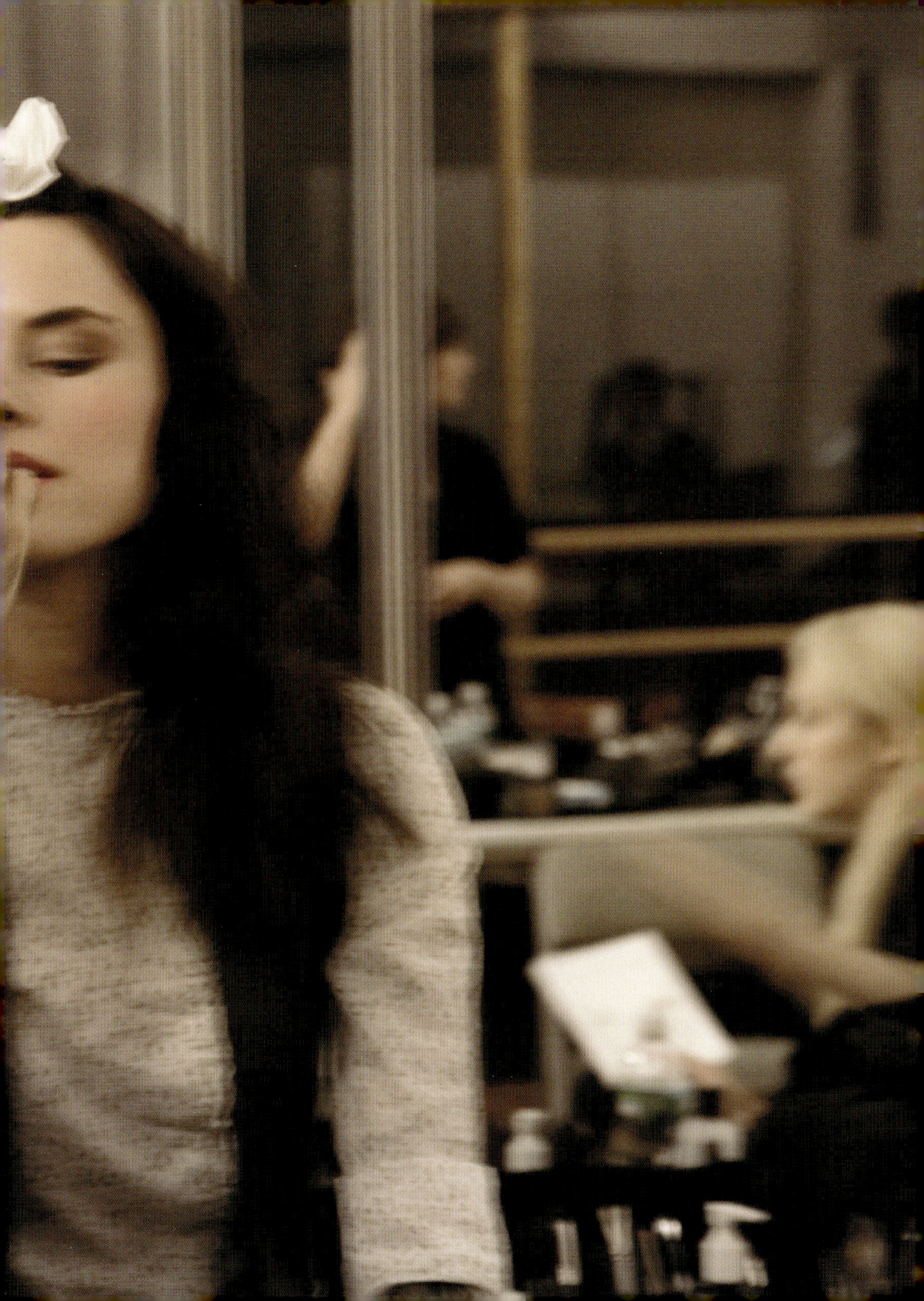

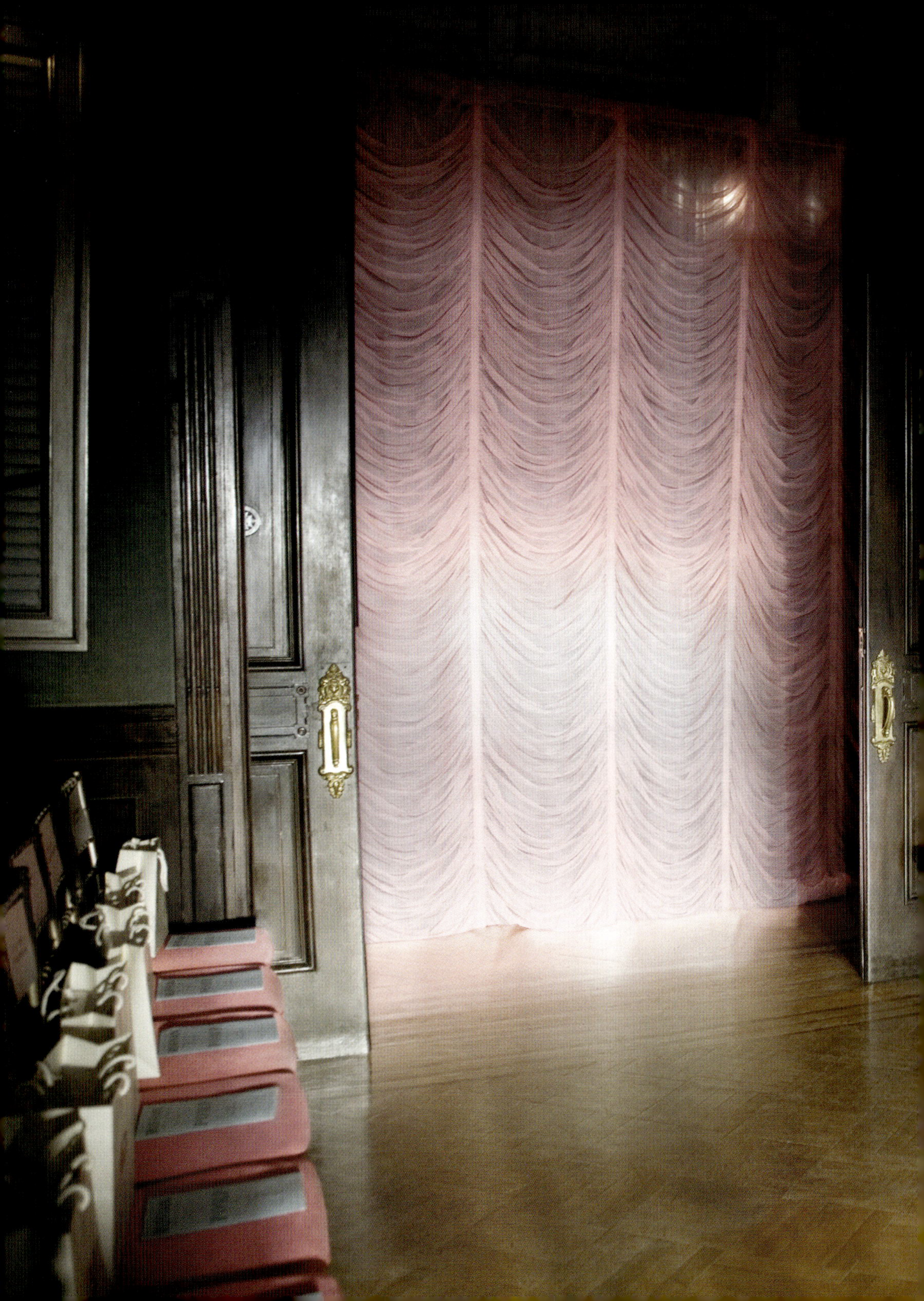

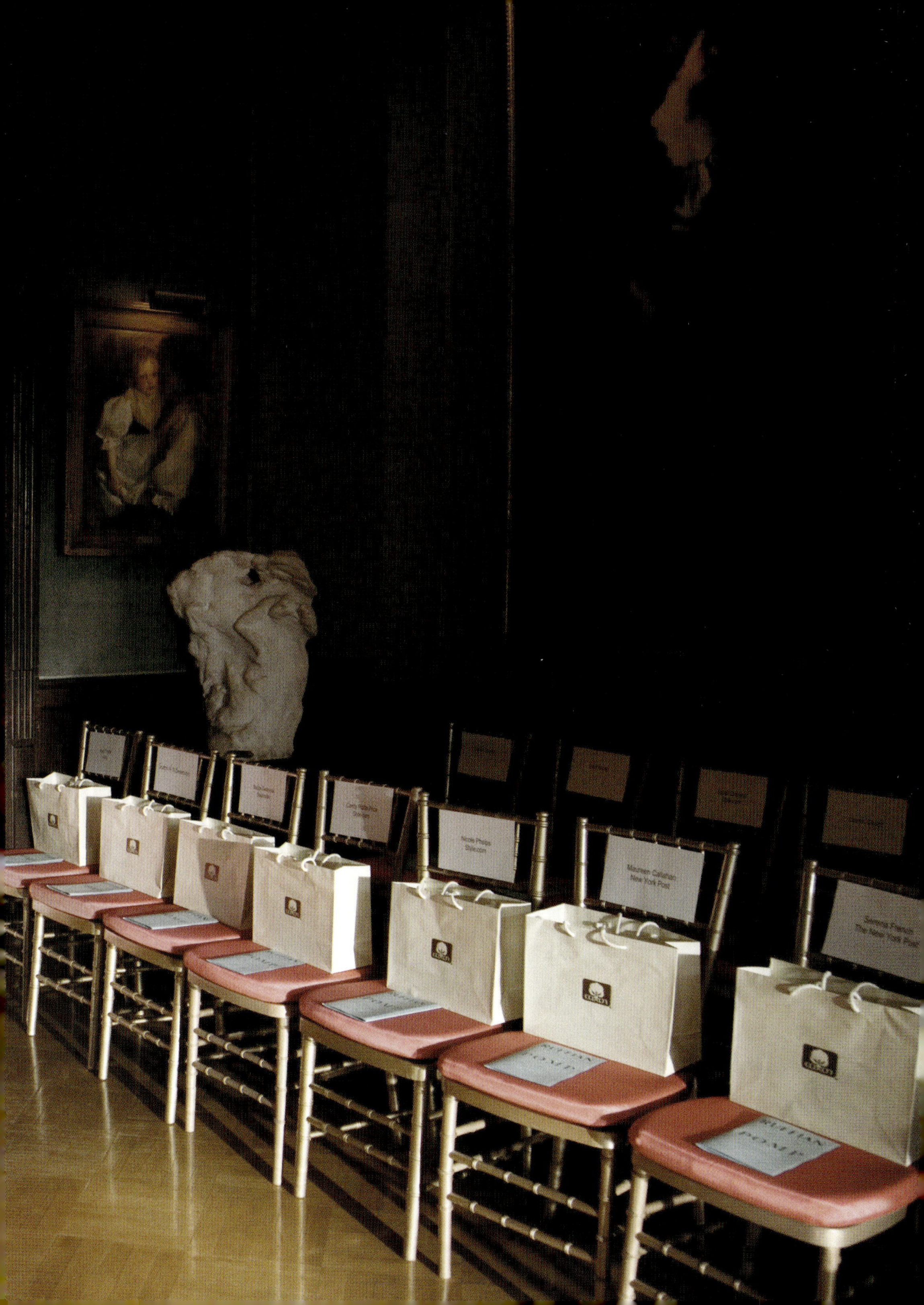

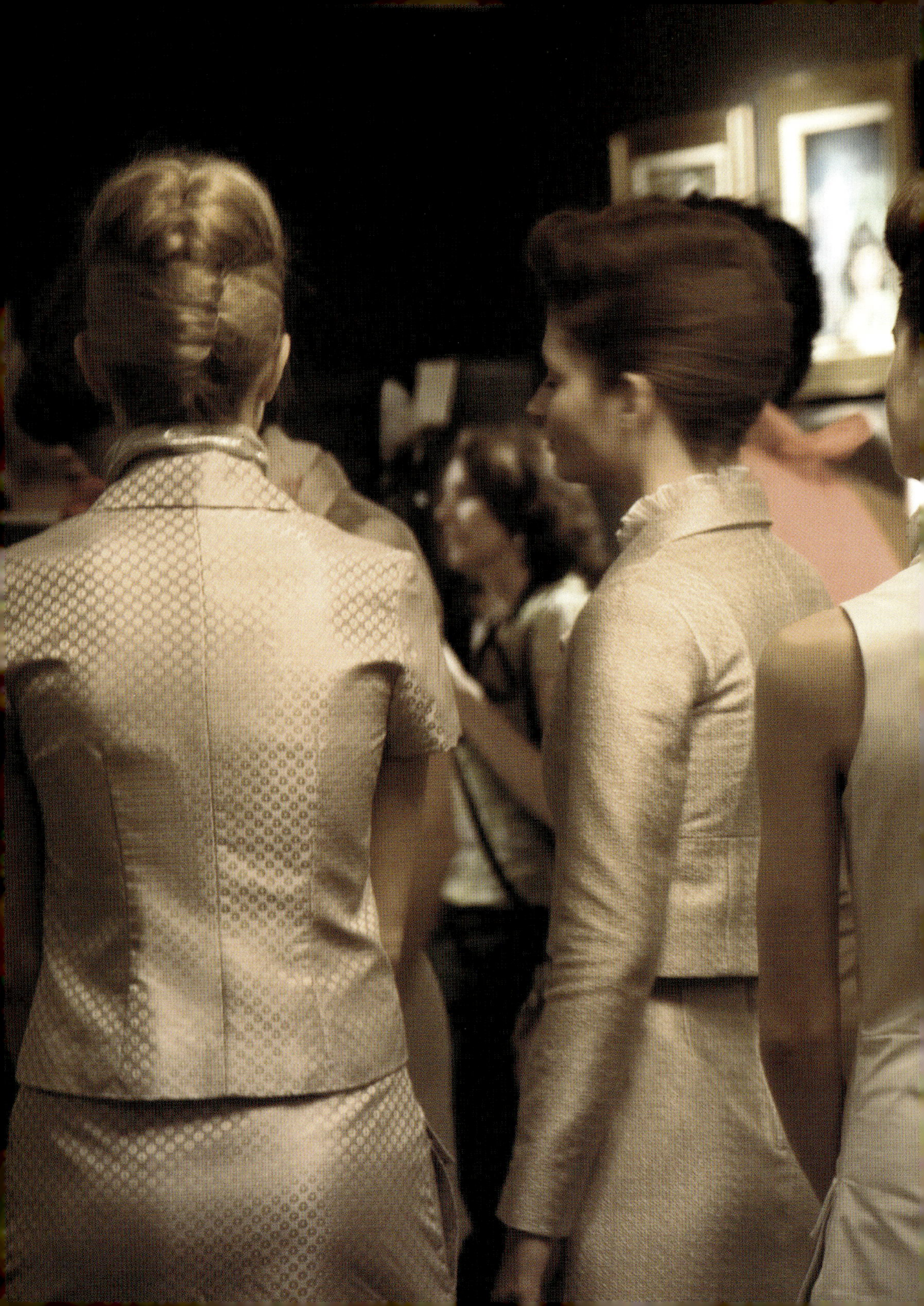

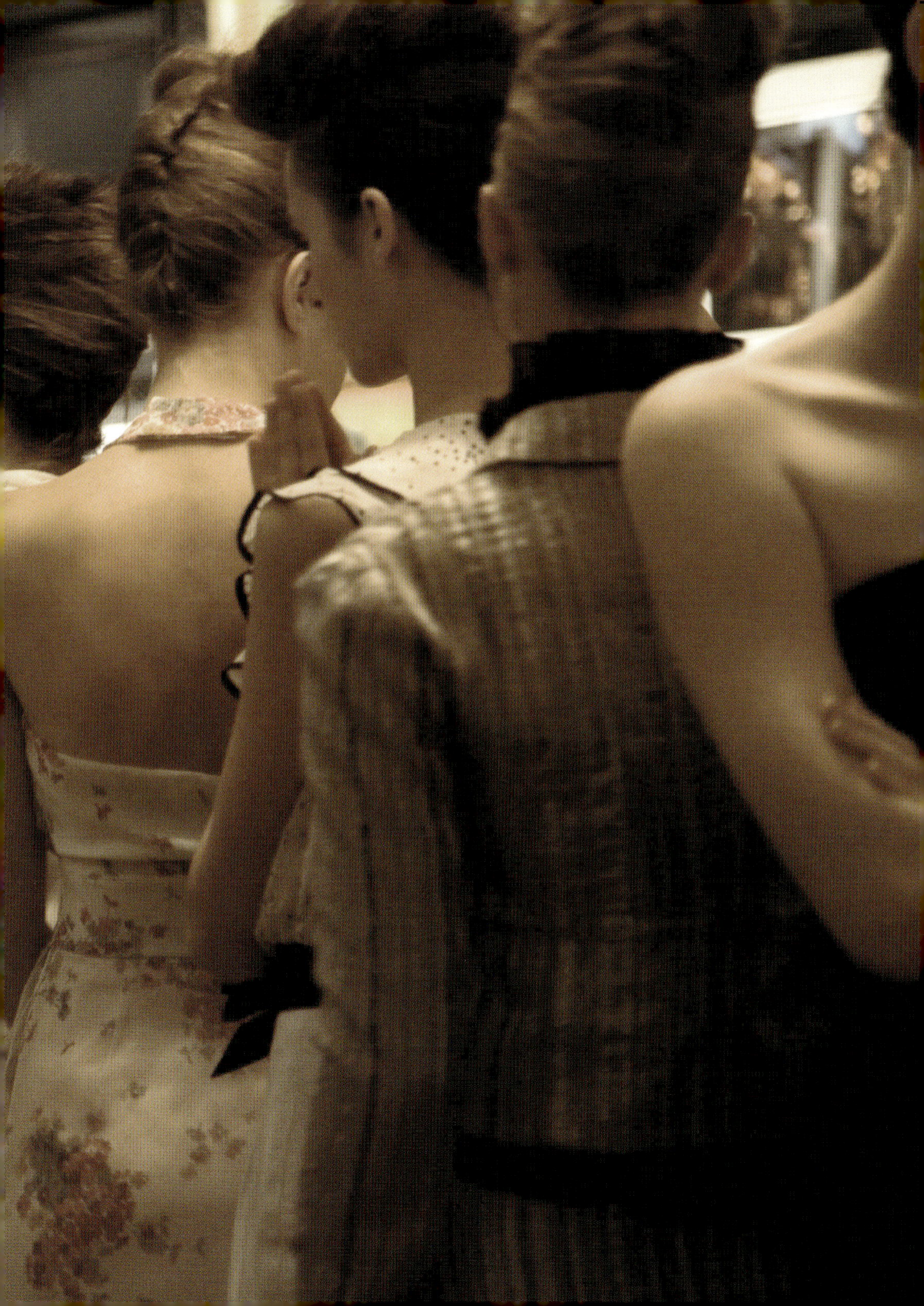

“Brian Wolk and Claude Morais have a rarefied vision.”

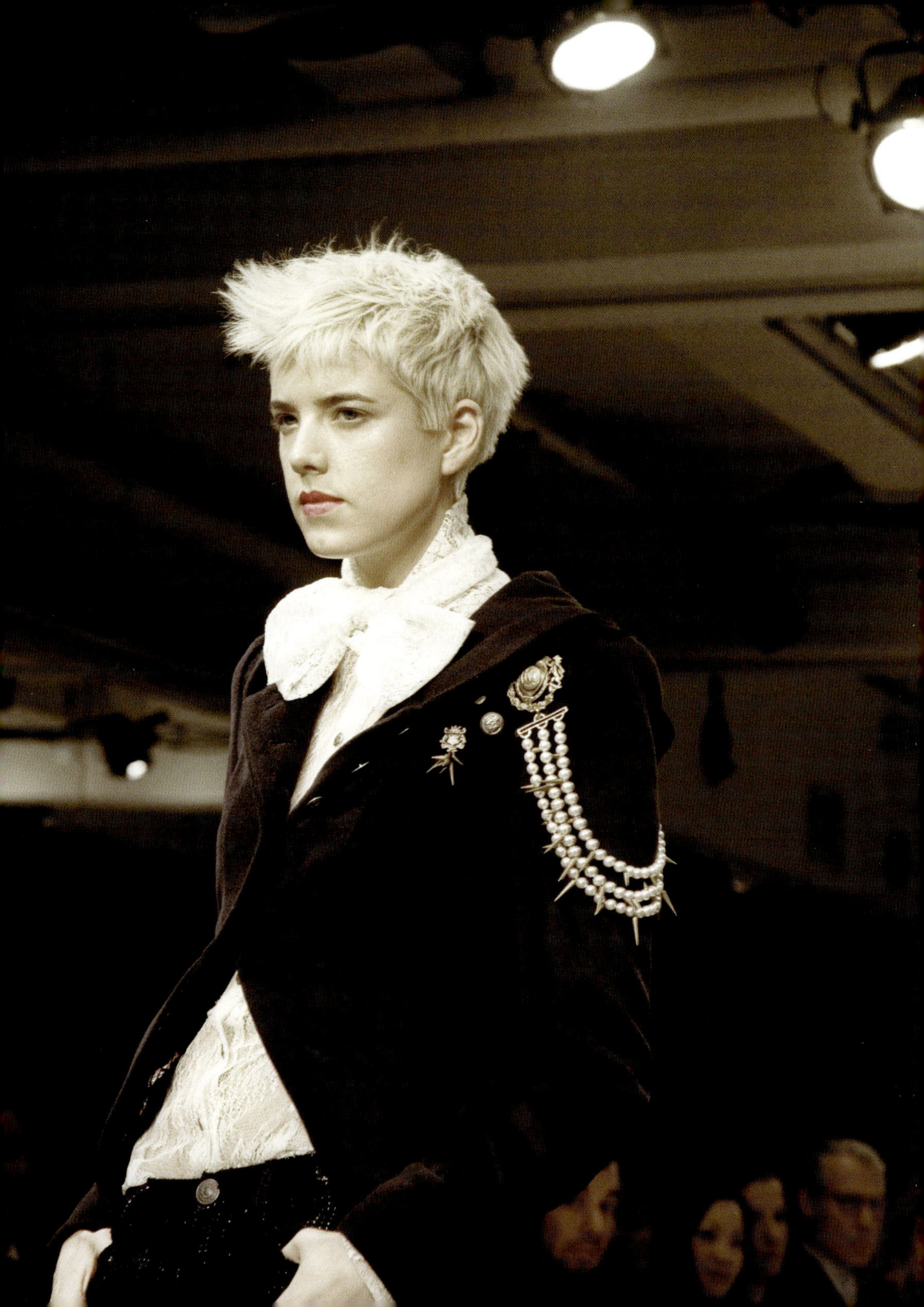

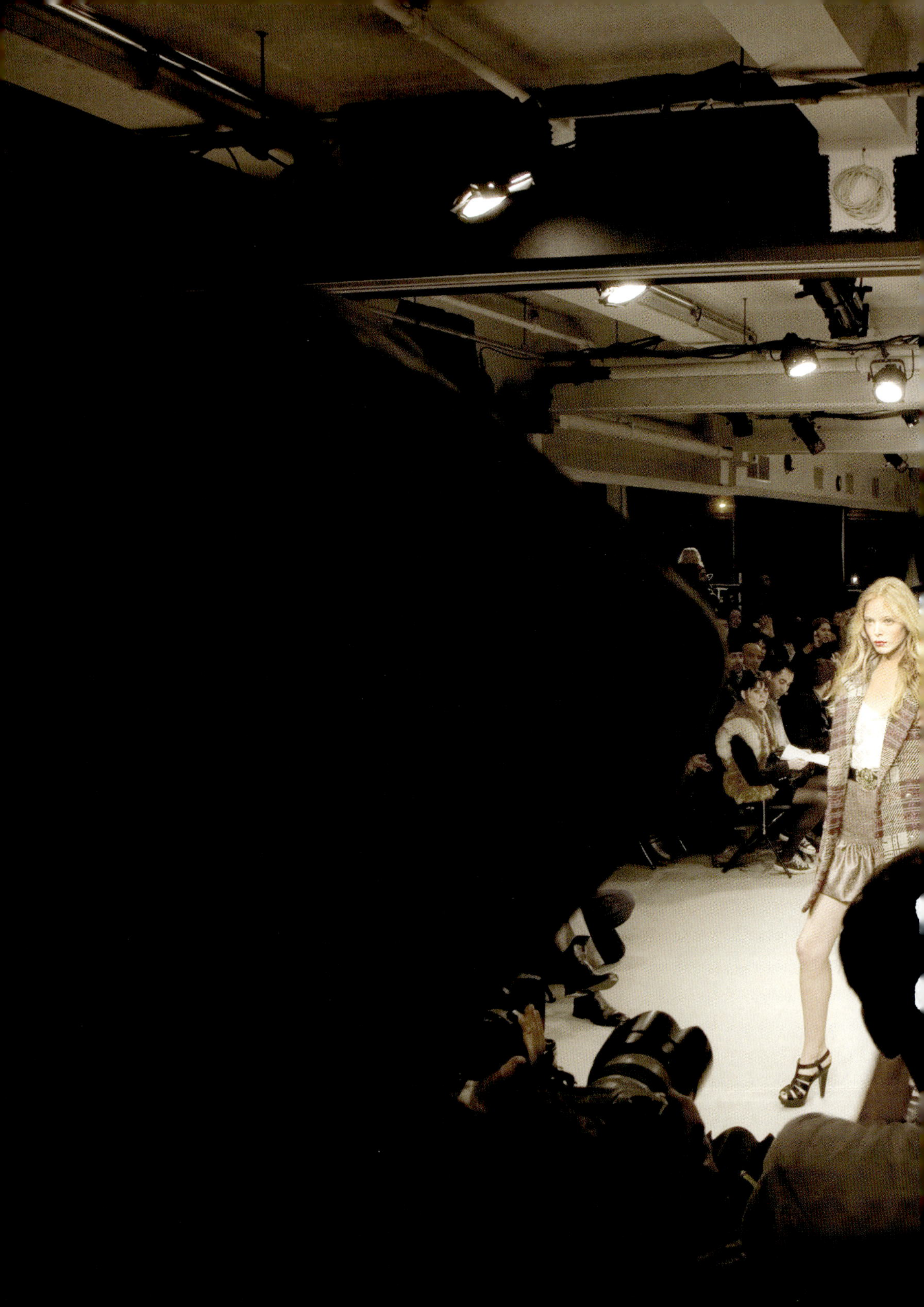

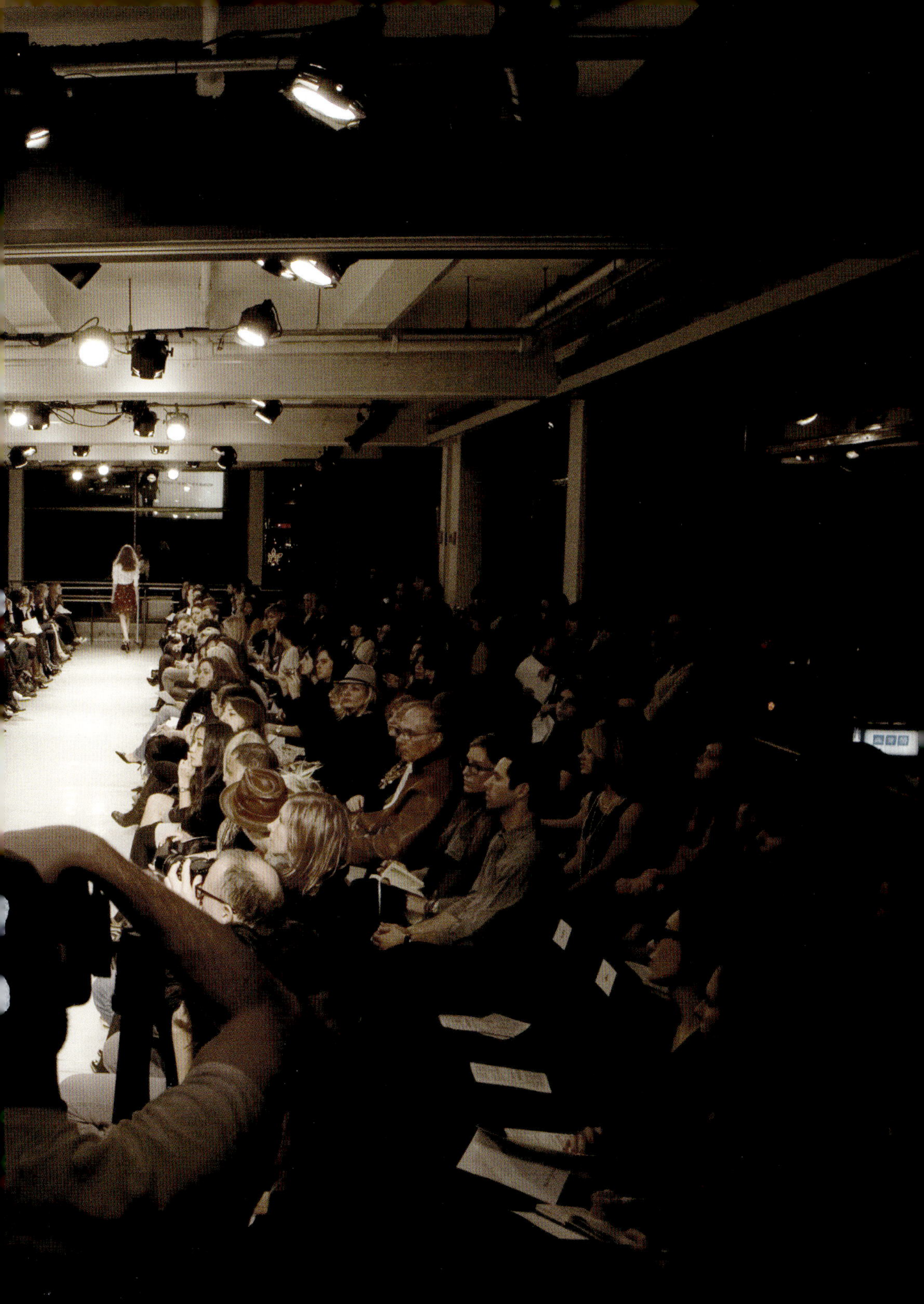

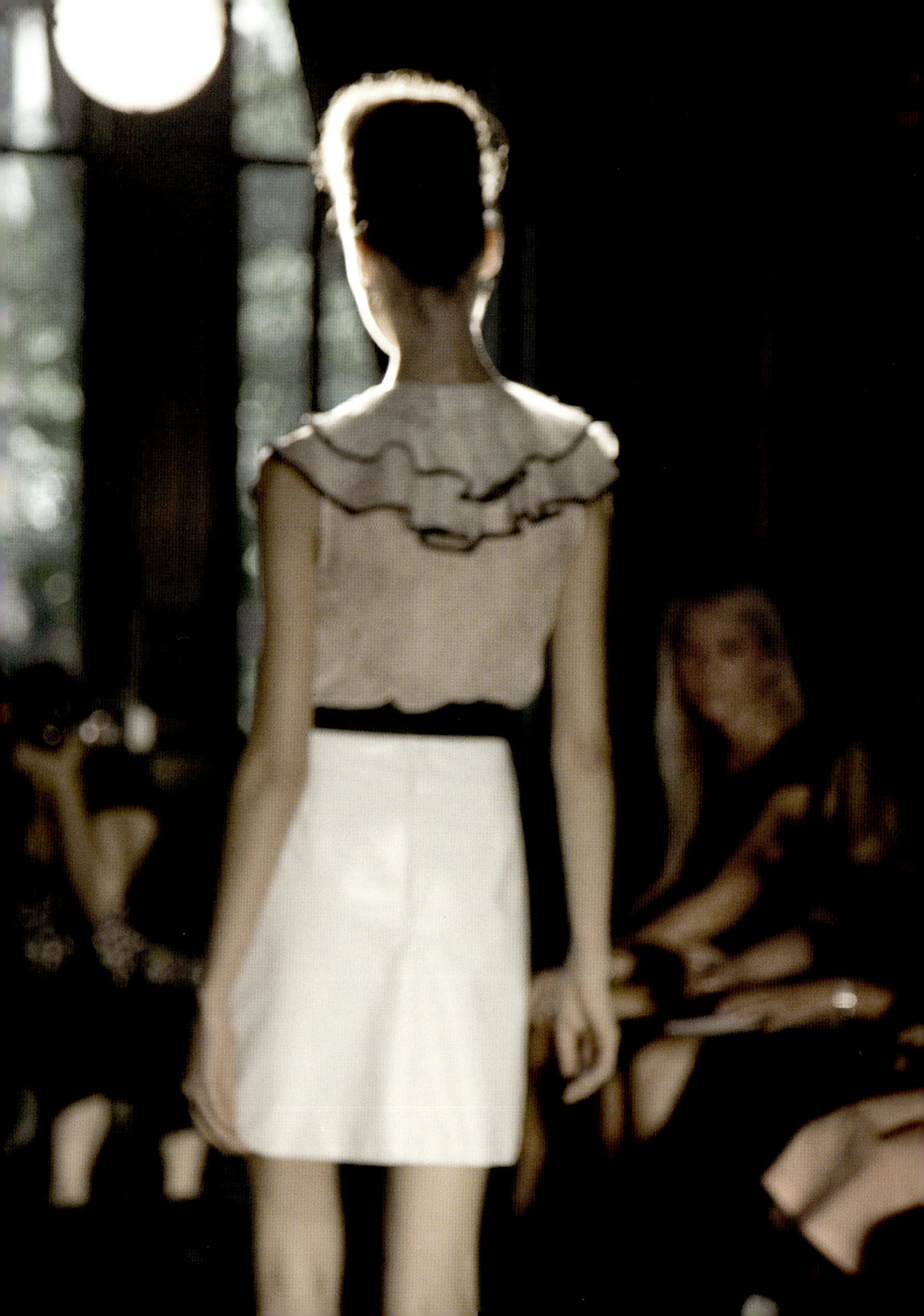

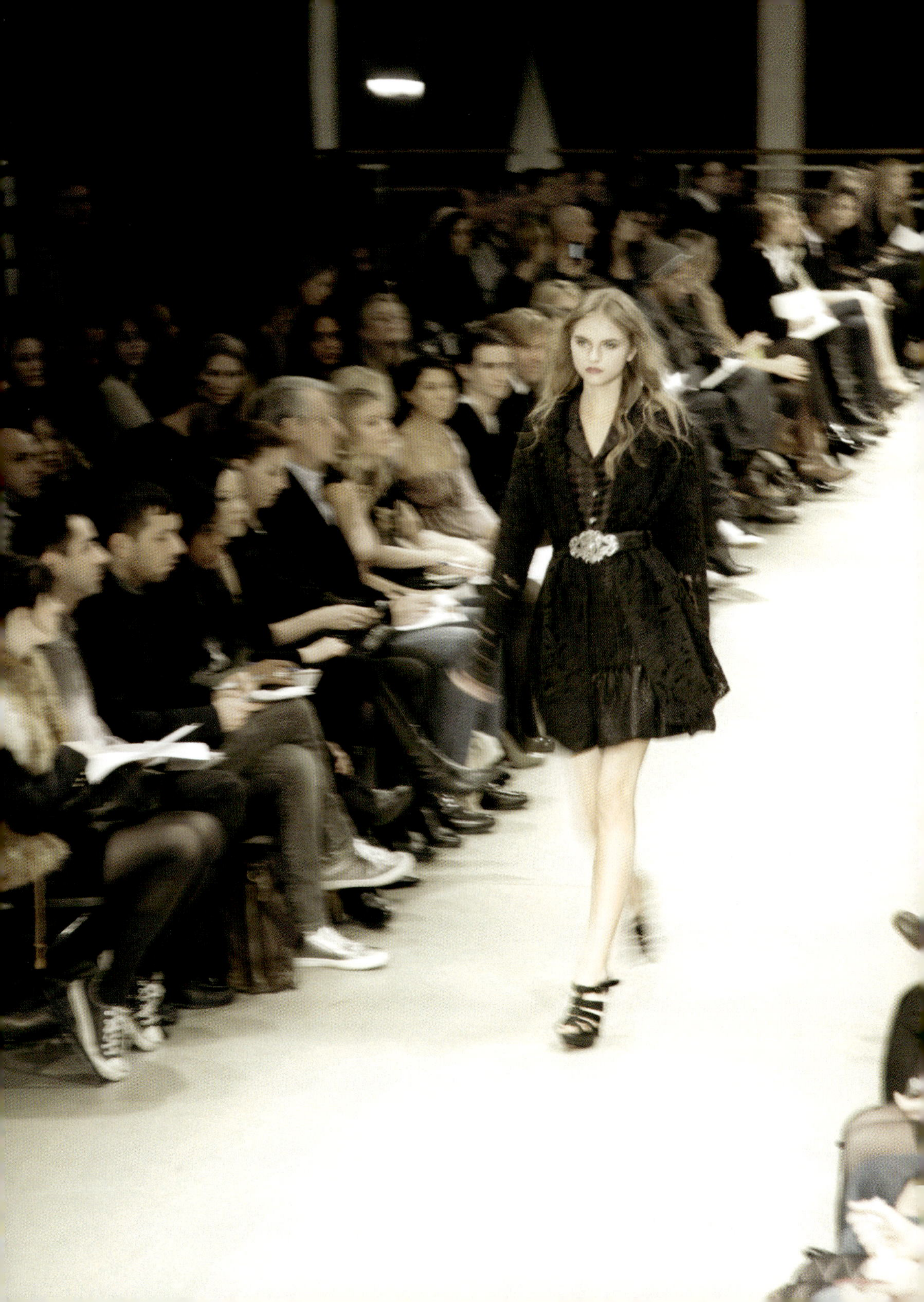

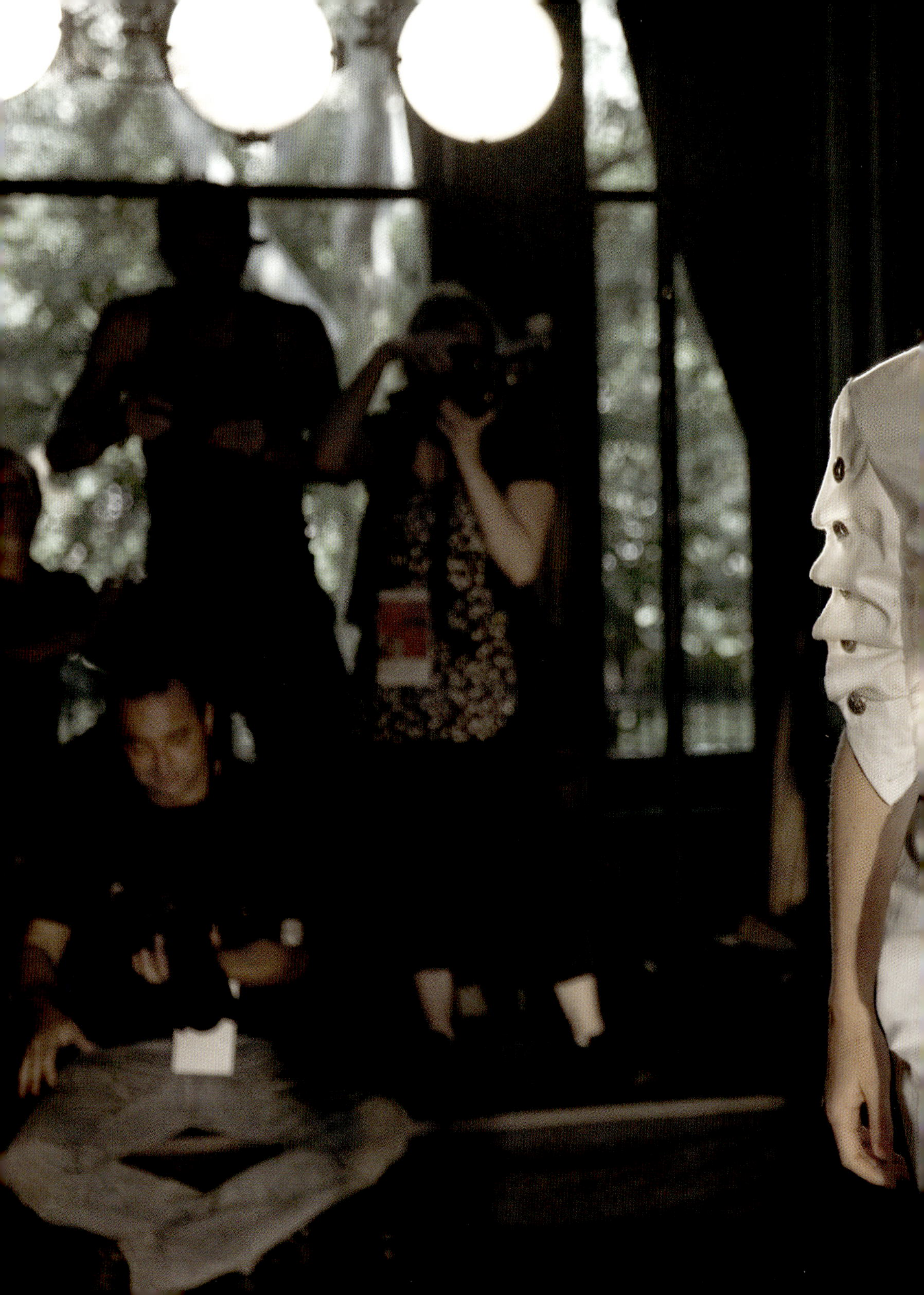

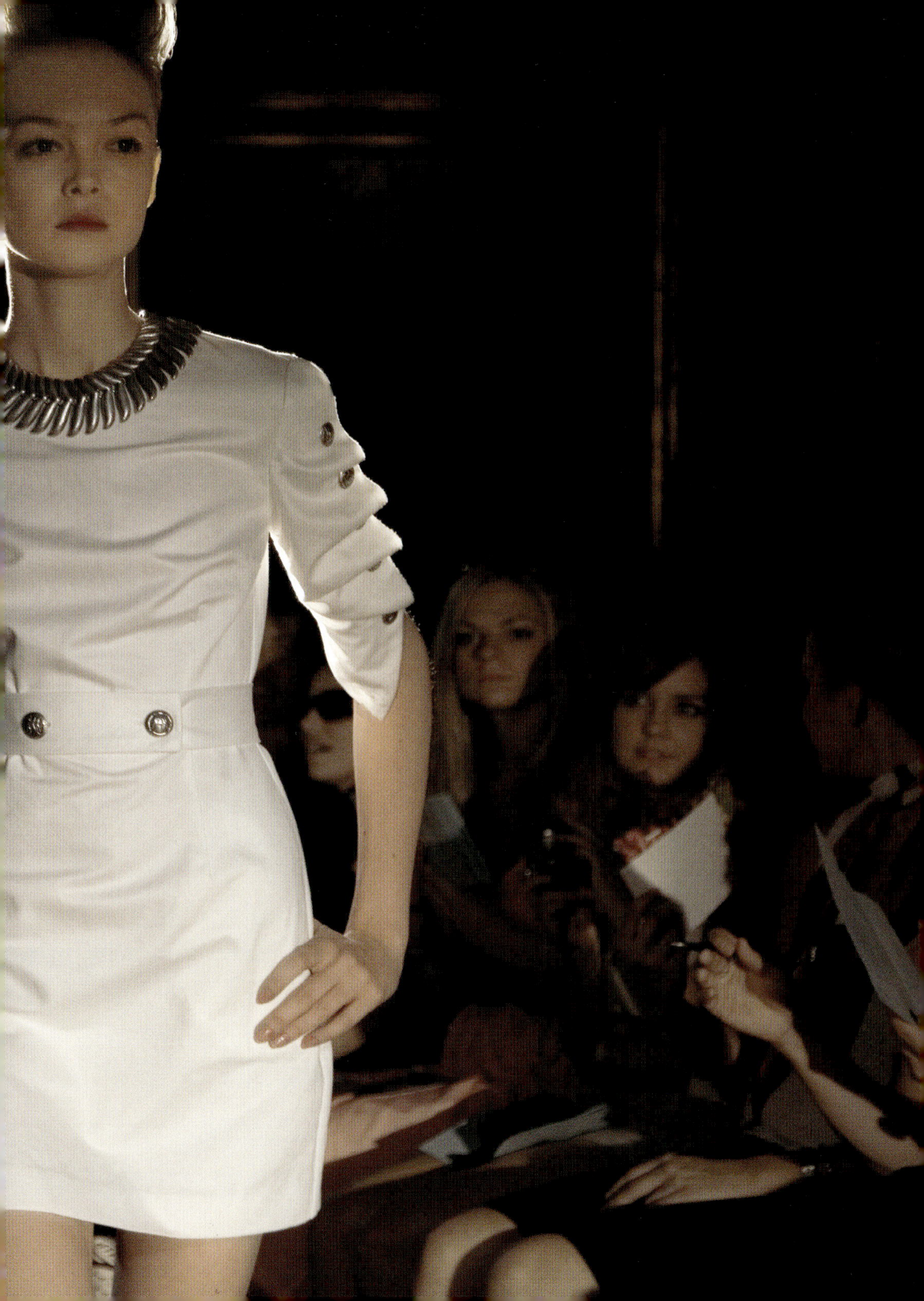

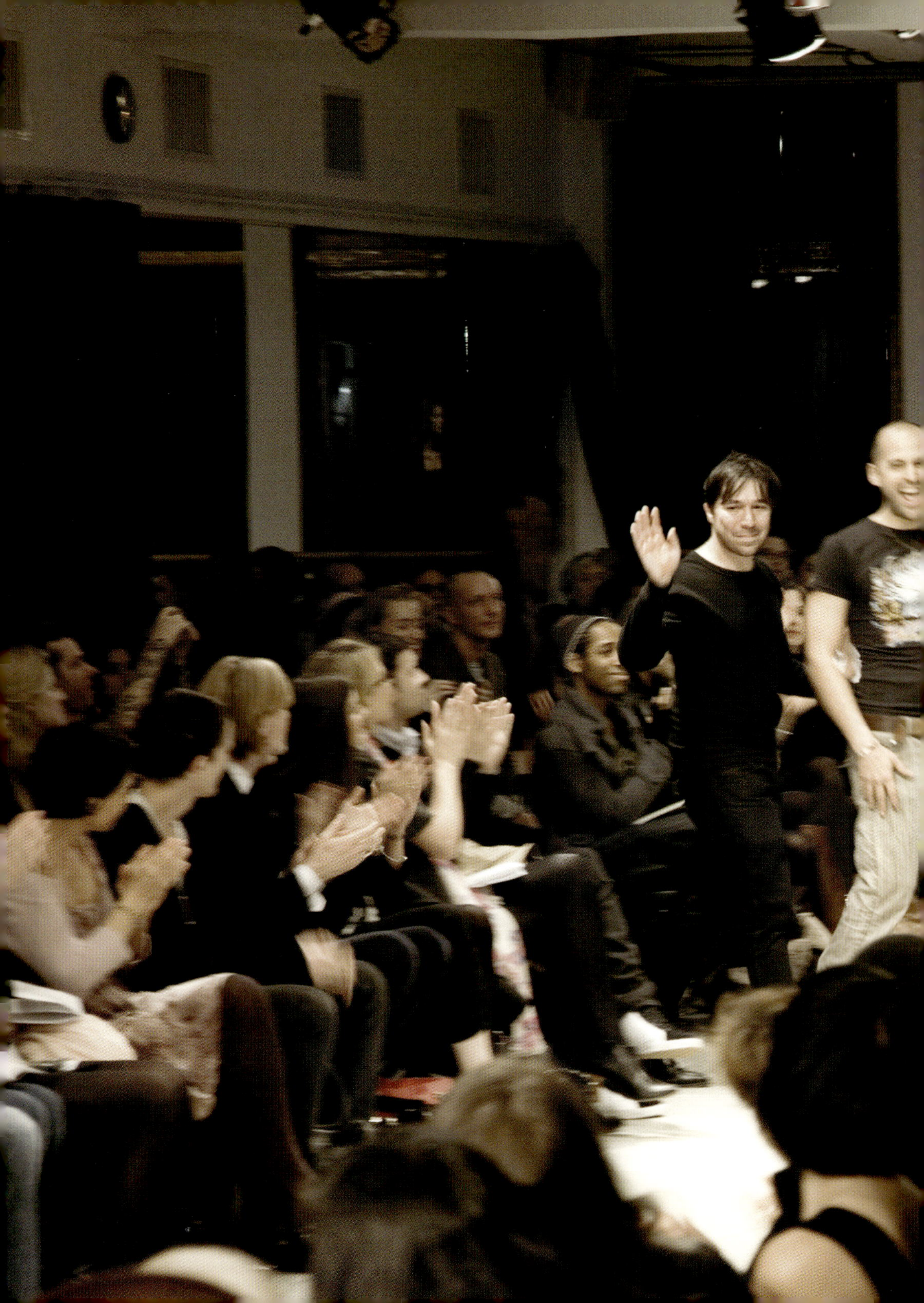

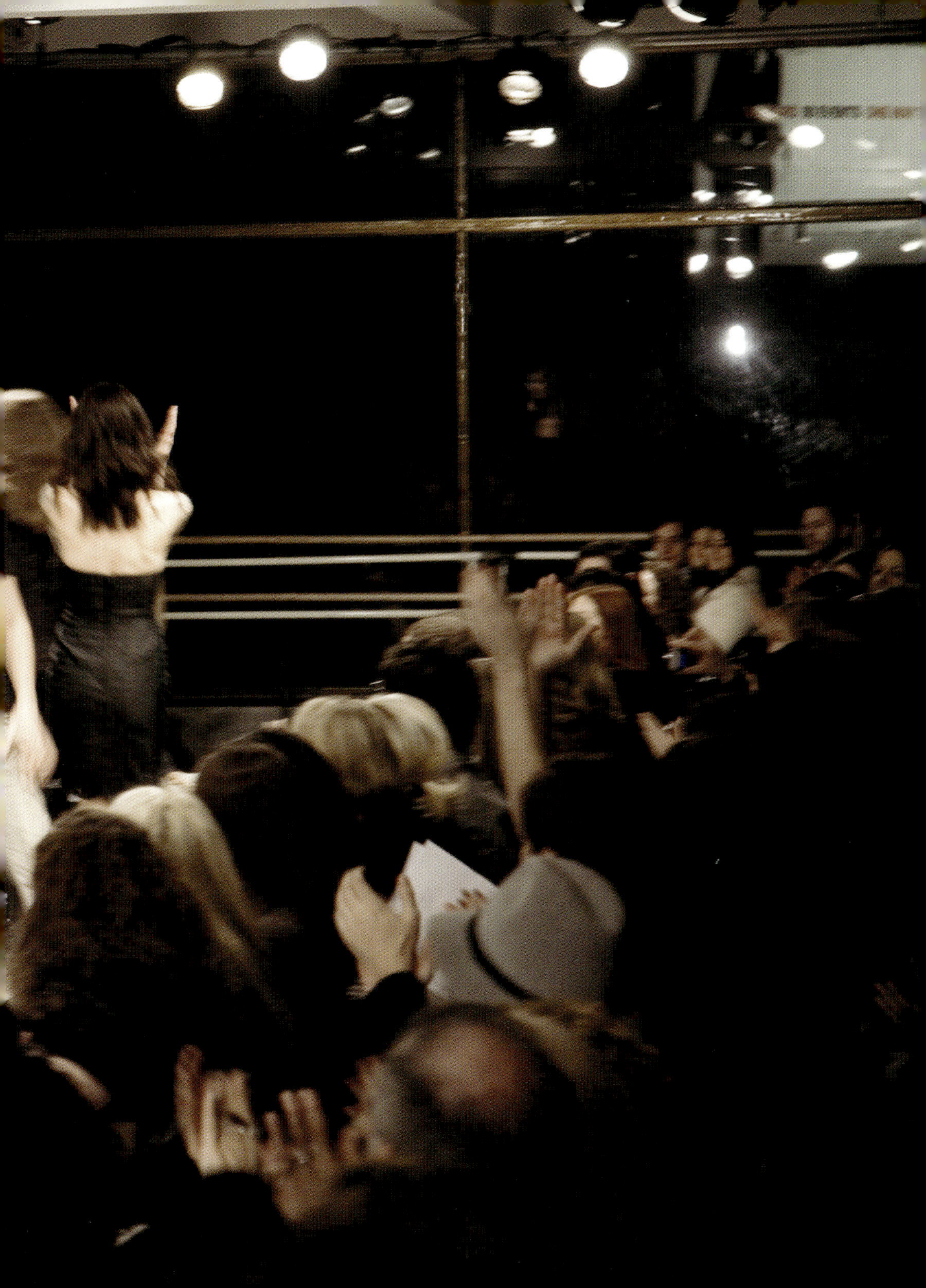

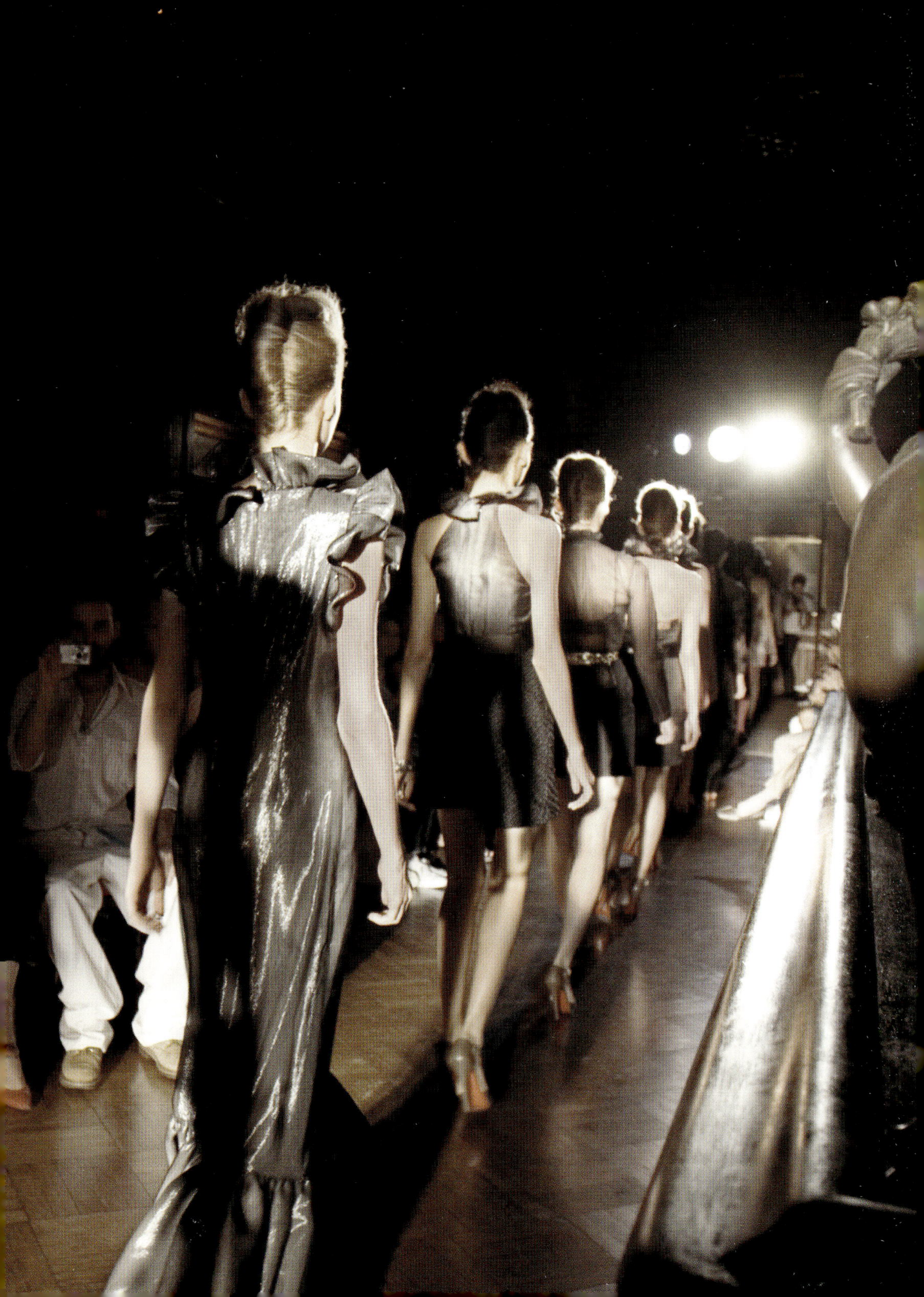

Chronology

73

1999:   Debut of Ruffian collars and neckpieces at a private residence near Gramercy Park.
Karl Lagerfeld photographs Cate Blanchett in a Ruffian collar for the December issue of *Harper's Bazaar.*

2000:   Barneys New York buys the collar collection and features one on the cover of its Accessory Book.
Ruffian introduces a line of men's couture neckwear, which is subsequently picked up by Barneys.

2002:   Ruffian shows its first collection of dresses at Beethoven Hall in New York, sponsored by Swarovski.

2003:   Ruffian brings its Savoy collection to London; Isabella Blow hosts tea and fashion show at namesake Savoy Hotel.
Ruffian shows the first of the American Trilogy, titled American Romantic, followed by American Novel and American Modern.
Ruffian begins collaboration with Christian Louboutin.

2004:   Ruffian moves into 306 West 38th Street studio in New York.

2006:   Ruffian wins Fashion Group International Rising Star Award.
Vogue magazine profiles Ruffian for the first time.

2007:   Ruffian opens doors in Moscow, Vienna, and Berlin.

2008:   Ruffian shows Pomp and (Re)form collections, expands its studio, and adds new gallery.

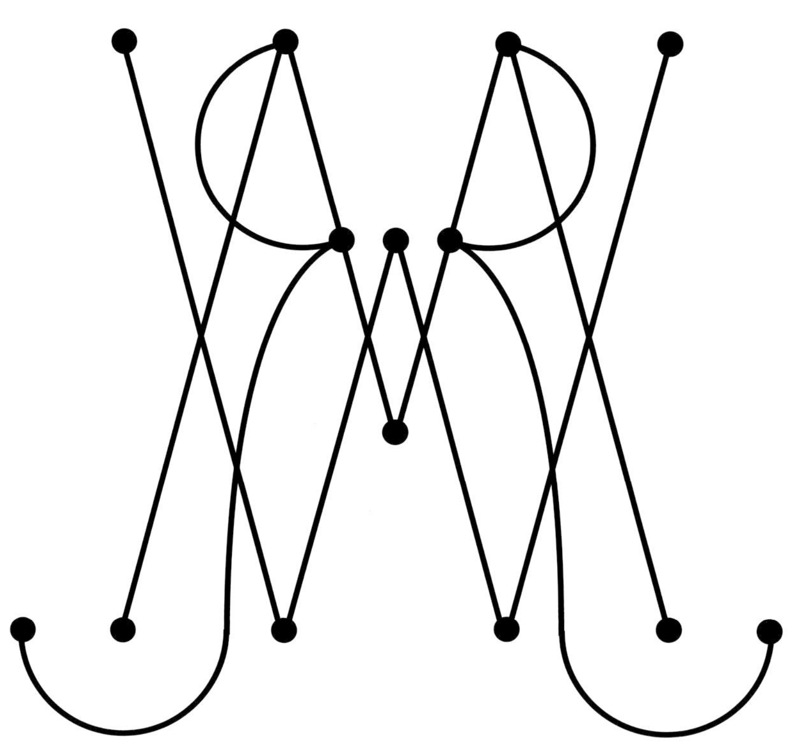

RUFFIAN

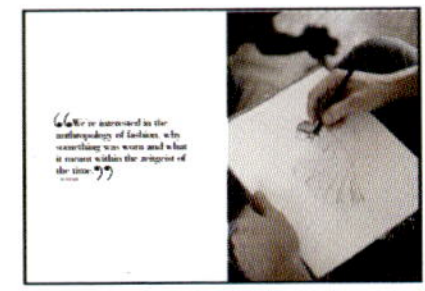

The beginning: First sketches of the fall 2008 (Re)form collection. Illustration by David Foote.

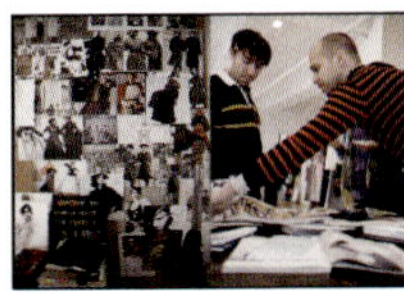

The inspiration board for the fall 2008 (Re)form collection, Ruffian Studio, New York.

Embroidery placement for fall 2008 (Re)form collection. Graffiti embroidery by needlepoint artist Heather Dunbar.

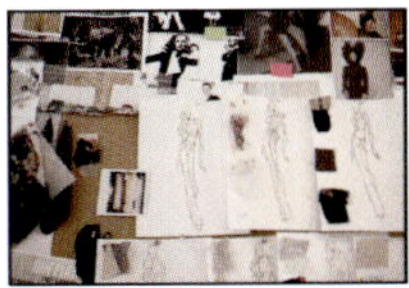

Look sketches for the spring 2008 Pomp collection. Illustration by David Foote.

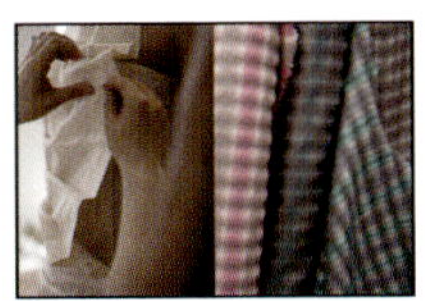

Draping of first muslin: Pomp, spring 2008.

Schoolgirl plaid: Fabric arrives from a mill in France, (Re)form, fall 2008.

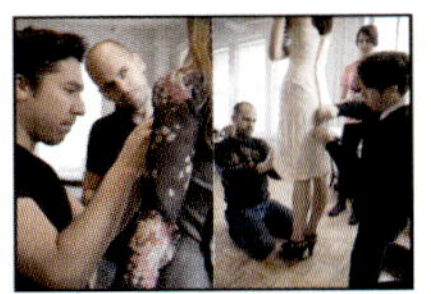

First fabric fitting for Pomp, spring 2008: Brian and Claude make alterations to an organza blouse.

Muslin fitting for (Re)form, fall 2008: Tailoring the muslin for the "Renee" dress.

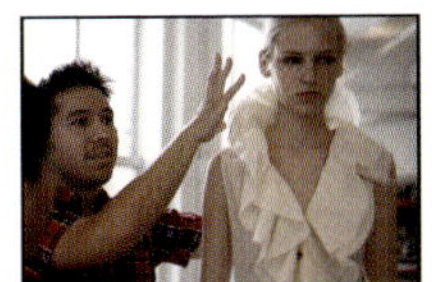

Architectural ruffles: Brian Wolk working out the proportion of a collar for Pomp, spring 2008.

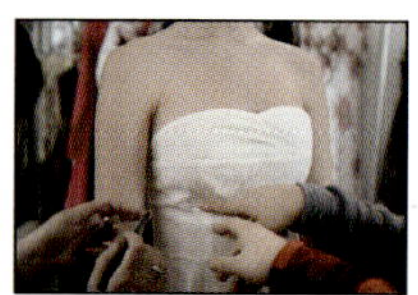

Perfect fit: Getting the fit perfected on a strapless dress for Pomp, spring 2008.

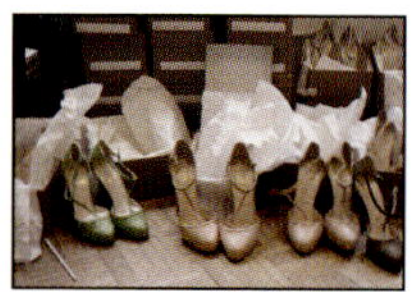

Heavenly soles: Custom Christian Louboutin shoes for Pomp, spring 2008, arrive from Paris.

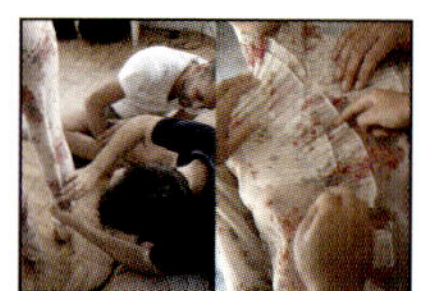

Sheer perfection: Fitting chiffon leggings for Pomp, spring 2008. **Pleating application** to the "Natasha" blouse, Pomp, spring 2008.

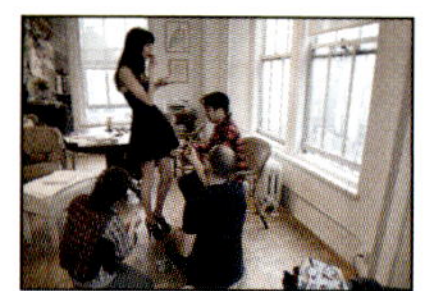

Sweet indulgence: Model Irina Lazareanu eats M & Ms while being fitted for her finale dress, (Re)form, fall 2008.

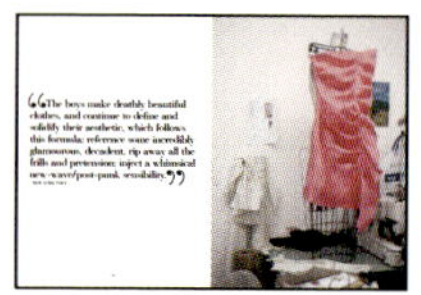

The **"One Wing Dove"** dress in the sample room the night before fitting, Pomp, spring 2008.

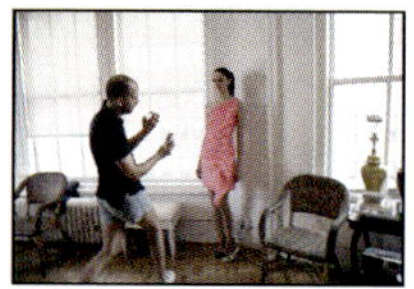

Taking flight: Lisa Cant at the final fitting in the "One Wing Dove" dress for Pomp, spring 2008.

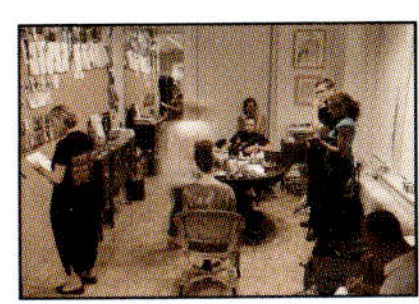

Hair and makeup test: Hairstylist Neil Moody creates the pompadour for Pomp, spring 2008.

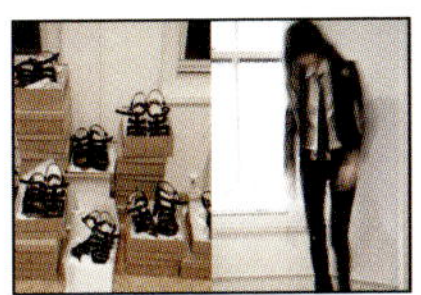

Killer sandals: Christian Louboutin pony sandals for (Re)form, fall 2008.
A "Muse"ment: Irina Lazareanu in slim suit at final fitting, (Re)form, fall 2008.

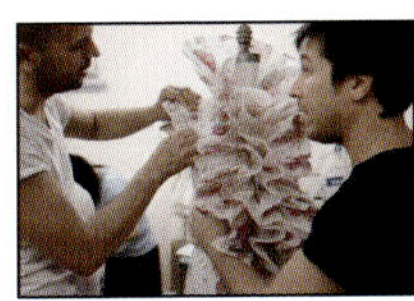

Finale dress: A waterfall of ruffles envelop the neckline on a dress the night before the show for Pomp, spring 2008.

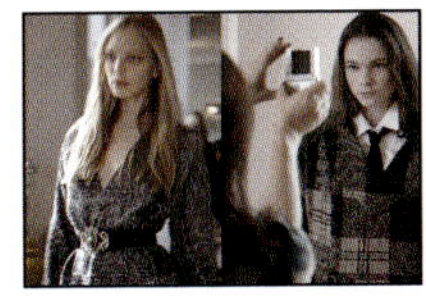

The "Baja" dress: Tanya in floor length French bouclé "Baja" dress, (Re)form, fall 2008.
Model student: Irina K. embodies boarding-school rebellion in shirt, tie, and plaid baja, (Re)form, fall 2008.

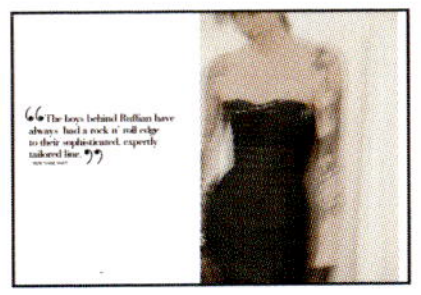

Second skin: Renee at the final fitting in a plaid French silk strapless dress, (Re)form, fall 2008.

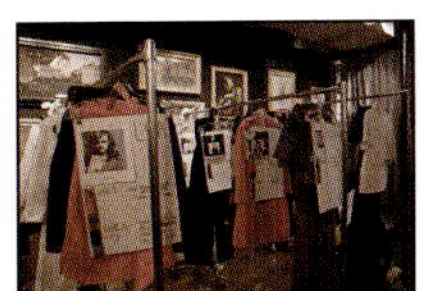

Dressing room: Racks backstage at the National Arts Club, New York, for presentation of Pomp, spring 2008.

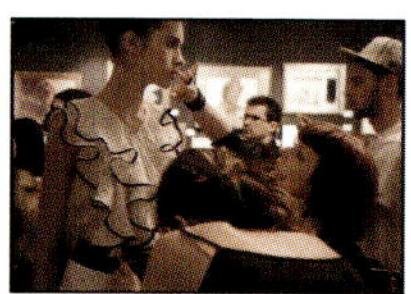

Touch-up: Maria R. getting a final touch-up before her runway exit, Pomp, spring 2008.

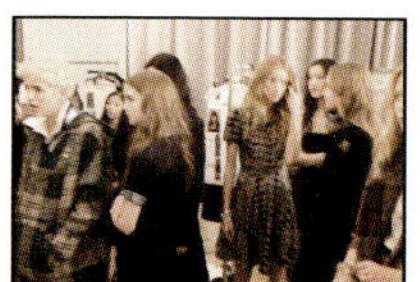

School for scandal: the "schoolgirls" line up backstage at New Dance Group Studios, (Re)form, fall 2008.

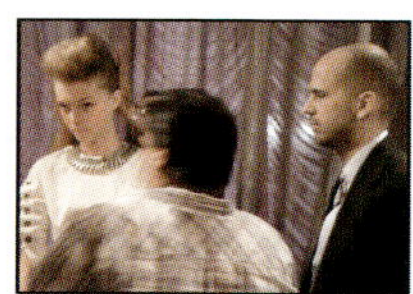

Expectant father: backstage, after much labor, Claude prepares for the birth of Pomp, spring 2008. Model: Siri.

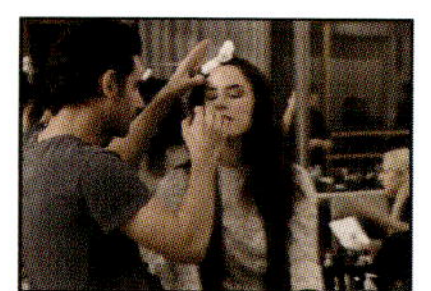

Eye contact: James Kaliardos applying makeup to model Renee backstage at (Re)form show, fall 2008.

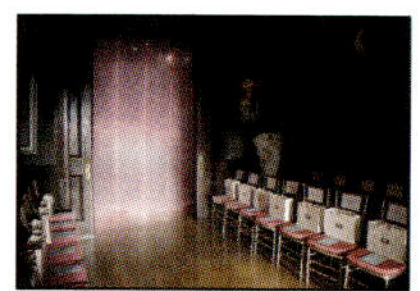

Curtain call: The National Arts Club on the morning of the show for Pomp, spring 2008.

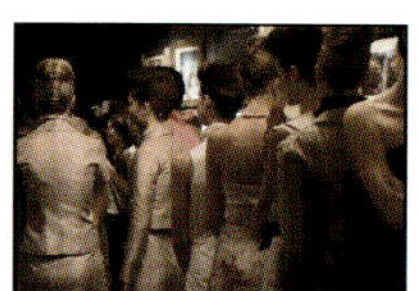

Up-dos: Models line up before going down runway, Pomp, spring 2008.

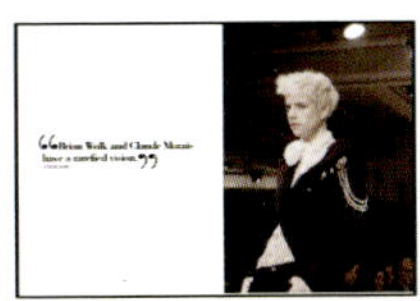

The Little Prince(ess): Agyness Deyn in cashmere coat, French lace blouse, and jewelry by Fenton for Ruffian, (Re)form, fall 2008.

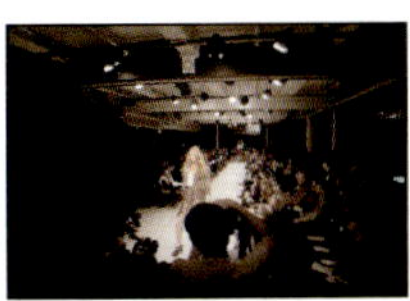

Photo finish: Tanya D. posing at the end of the runway at New Dance Group Studios, (Re)form, fall 2008.

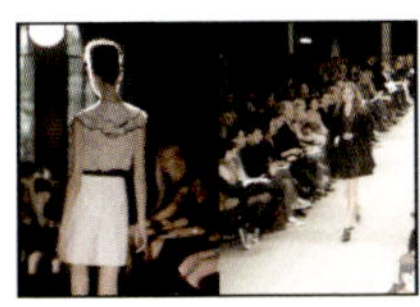

Leather and lace: Bouclé crocodile skirt and French lace blouse on Du Juan, (Re)form, fall 2008.
Hard edges: A piped, ruffled, polka-dot chiffon blouse and leather skirt from Pomp, spring 2008.

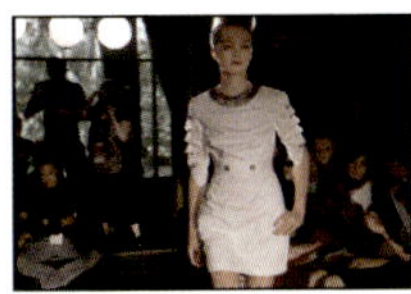

Buttoned up: Siri in signature button-sleeved, waxed Japanese cotton dress and necklace by Fenton for Ruffian, Pomp, spring 2008.

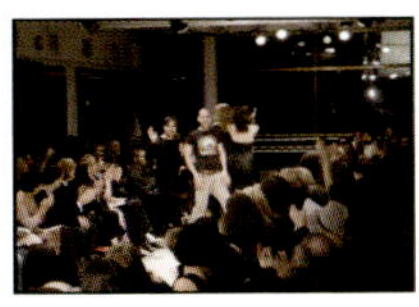

Take a bow: Brian Wolk and Claude Morais wrap up the show of (Re)form, fall 2008.

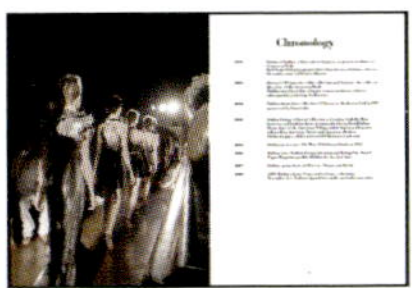

Pomp and circumstance: Models do their finale parade at the National Arts Club, Pomp, spring 2008.

Acknowledgments

The designers wish to thank the following people for their contributions to this book: Lee Wolk, Dr. Allan Wolk and Iris Wolk, Line Boulianne, Crystal Kim, Angela Panichi, Angelica Compagno, Aldon James and the National Arts Club, Anne Koch, Antonia Thompson, Charity Guzofski, Christian Louboutin, David Foote, Dayna Zegarelli, Dana Lorenz, Eloise Danch, Hugo Marchand, Isabella Blow, James Kaliardos, Jane Keltner, Katherine Ensslen, Kwok Chan, Lindsay Thompson, Liz Jin, Maggie Norris, Mary Nelson Sinclair, Max Pasquier, Nadja Swarovski, Natasha Royt, Neil Moody, Nelson Silva, Nicole Phelps, Polly Osmond, Rena Lazaros, Renee Dorski, Sabine Heller, Shawn Steiner, Shawna Rose, Susan Macintosh, the Zagoreos family, Tim Rush, Todd Bagwell, Art + Commerce, Bumble & bumble, Cotton Inc., and M.A.C.

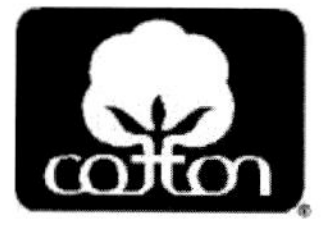